IT HAPPENED IN
SAN FRANCISCO

Maxine Cass

TWODOT®

GUILFORD, CONNECTICUT
HELENA, MONTANA
AN IMPRINT OF THE GLOBE PEQUOT PRESS

A · T W O D O T® · B O O K

Front cover: Golden Gate Bridge under construction. Library of Congress,
LC-USZ62-100678
Back cover: The Cliff House burning. Library of Congress, LC-USZ62-105764
Text design by Nancy Freeborn
Map by M.A. Dubé © Morris Book Publishing, LLC

Library of Congress Cataloging-in-Publication Data
Cass, Maxine.
   It happened in San Francisco/Maxine Cass.—1st ed.
       p. cm.—(It happened in)
   Includes bibliographical references and index.
   ISBN 0-7627-3823-5
   1. San Francisco (Calif.)—History—Anecdotes. I. Title. II. It happened in series.
F869.S357C37 2006
979.4'61—dc22
                                                                    2005023243

Manufactured in the United States of America
First Edition/First Printing

For Jackie O'Leary-Kroenung and love to
Fred Gebhart, Mendo, and the Chocolate Panther.

CONTENTS

CONTENTS

ACKNOWLEDGMENTS

Endless thanks are due to Laurie Armstrong of the San Francisco Convention & Visitors Bureau; Steve Giordano; Bob Grimes and his San Francisco music collection; Virginia McCarthy; internment survivor, Haruko "Holly" Nakama; Ben Rodriguez; Laura del Rosso; Manny, Danny, Nelly, and Bob at the Parkside U.S. Post Office; the National Park Service; the San Francisco Public Library; San Francisco history doyenne, Gladys Hansen; and the resources of the Virtual Museum of the City of San Francisco.

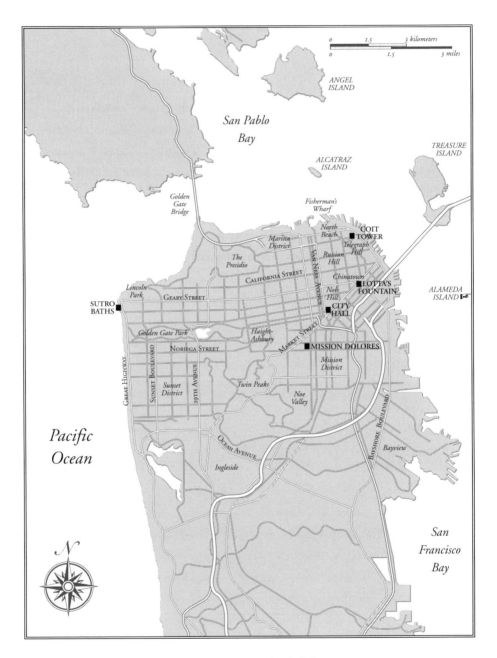

SAN FRANCISCO

INTRODUCTION

SAN FRANCISCO, AT THE WESTERN EDGE of a mighty continent, is blessed with an attractive location, colorful characters, and fabled icons like cable cars and the Golden Gate Bridge. It is publicized internationally in films and books and by its signature song, *I Left My Heart in San Francisco*. It's a compact, walkable city that nevertheless challenges visitors with its hills.

It's also a city where residents survive and thrive in distinct neighborhoods and where tourism is the number one industry. Historic and famous Chinatown is matched by two lesser-known "Chinatowns" in west San Francisco's Richmond and Sunset Districts. Italians whose grandparents originally emigrated from Sicily or Lucca still live and work in North Beach. The Mission District, the city's sunny central heart, is traditionally the first stop for immigrants, though Hispanics have been in the neighborhood since Spaniards established Mission Dolores there in 1776.

San Francisco's history and lively personalities have often been offbeat and out of sync with the rest of the country. With the Gold Rush came a sense that anything was possible and that social change could happen. Some events were violent, but social change just as often came with new ideas and forward-thinking entrepreneurs looking to turn inventions into money-making projects. Politics are often liberal on the battleground between forward thinkers and others whose outside-the-box ideas border on outlandish. San Franciscans are proud of their best-known crackpot, Emperor Norton, whose nineteenth-century proclamations were surprisingly tolerant of a racial diversity that also included his prophetic demand for a bridge to span San Francisco Bay. Another example of San Francisco's liberal idealism continues today;

in 2004, Mayor Gavin Newsom authorized the city hall registrar to marry same-gender couples.

The first Spaniards to set eyes on the bay, hills, and marshlands in the 1770s were determined people—fog, damp, and lack of provisions wouldn't deter their settlement. After gold was discovered northeast of the tiny bayside settlement in 1848, within only a few months thousands of prospectors flowed through San Francisco to follow hopeful goldfield dreams. Many of the real Gold Rush success stories were of businessmen like fourteen-year-old baker Isidore Boudin, wholesale merchant Sam Brannan, and trouser-maker Levi Strauss. Other locals weathered blatant racial discrimination to succeed—like the Chinese immigrants who laundered prospectors' clothes and built the Transcontinental Railroad for Nevada Comstock Lode silver barons. Those men in turn built opulent mansions on the top of Nob Hill.

San Francisco's more colorful characters included Scotsman Andrew Hallidie, whose technology for a cable car solved access to the city's steep hills. Lillie Hitchcock Coit's childhood fire-engine chasing earned her mascot status and a nozzle-shaped monument atop Telegraph Hill where, 150 years later, Mark Bittner encountered and loved a flock of wild parrots. Longshoreman labor activist Harry Bridges reformed the waterfront and United States labor laws with the 1934 General Strike that followed Bloody Thursday. Poet Allen Ginsberg read his beat-era *Howl* as protest against the Cold War. A decade later Haight-Ashbury hippies were wearing flowers, peace signs, and reveling in the Summer of Love.

Nothing shaped San Francisco more than the earthquakes and fires that rocked, rolled, and repeatedly burned the city. In 1865 Mark Twain's *Earthquake Almanac* wryly described "spasmodic but exhilarating earthquakes, accompanied by occasional showers of rain, and churches and things." The 1906 Earthquake shook for a minute in the early hours of an April day. A mighty temblor, it caused building frames, plaster, and streets to tumble into rubble, only to be followed by fires and dynamiting for firebreaks. The violence that left thousands of homeless camping in the parks forced San Francisco to rebuild, clean up political corruption, and show the world what the city's symbol of a phoenix rising from the flames really meant.

The 1906 Earthquake and Fire and the 1989 Loma Prieta Quake are history, but San Franciscans live with earthquakes and their legacy every day. Many of the monuments and attitudes from former eras are incorporated into the city's fabric and psyche. "Stuff in our lifetime is history already?" my San Francisco-born friend, Steve Giordano, asked recently.

It's easy to breathe the city's history while living here. I took a cable car to school before it became a popular tourist attraction. The former bank building where Patty Hearst participated in a 1974 "political" robbery is not far from my home. Old-time San Franciscans are puzzled over the popular Alcatraz Island tours—after all, it was a federal penitentiary, and no one *wanted* to go there.

Many San Franciscans had gold-prospector forbearers. My own Danish immigrant grandfather, whose only souvenir from the 1906 Earthquake was a cracked and fire-glazed cream pitcher, sang with Enrico Caruso, according to family stories. My husband and I lived in the heart of San Francisco's Castro District, ground zero for the West Coast's gay rights movement, for ten years.

As I write this in San Francisco's Sunset District, its third Chinatown, I have only to walk down the front steps to feel the cool breeze mixed with summer fog. I sniff the air, and the odors from my neighborhood's Chinese, Mexican, Thai, and Japanese restaurants fill my senses with desire. I shop at a Persian greengrocer, where produce stockers from Mexico and El Salvador bop and sway to alternating belly dance rhythms and Mexican Norteño ballads. A few doors down, barbecued duck, live crabs, and swimming fish are sold along-side bok choy and bitter long beans. The languages in my neighbor-hood are a swirl of four Chinese Cantonese dialects, plus Mandarin, Japanese, Spanish, Russian, Italian, Thai, French, and English. The speakers of many tongues are adding their own history and charac-ters to the local scene.

Enriched by frequent immigrant tides, this great western city sprung up from a gold rush and has barely looked back since. Residents and visitors alike enjoy a bracing walk across the Golden Gate Bridge to look back at the skyline view. Frilly Victorian mansions laced with gingerbread details in their architecture and classic cable cars climbing halfway to the proverbial stars are there. Beyond all of its icons, San Francisco is a nuanced, diverse city where history is made anew each day on its streets and hills.

CATTLE DRIVE

- 1776 -

On July 4, 1776, the Continental Congress declared the independence of the United States of America from British rule. One week earlier, oblivious to the actions of feisty colonists a continent away, Ensign José Joaquin Moraga founded Spain's newest colonial outpost. His eight-month-long cattle drive was finished.

Captain Juan Bautista de Anza, explorer and Apache fighter, had led 302 cattle and 240 people on an overland route from Tubac, in the Sonora region of Mexico, to San Diego and Monterey. The group included Moraga, soldiers and their wives, settlers, muleteers, cowboys, Indian interpreters, priests, servants, and children.

For poor settlers, the San Francisco settlement was an opportunity for land and prosperity. For soldiers, career advancement and land grants sweetened the duty. And the priests would extend their chain of missions north to convert Indian nonbelievers.

Anza had explored the route from Tubac (in what would later be southern Arizona) to the Royal Presidio of Monterey the year before.

This time Anza was determined to find the bay north of Monterey that he had heard was often shrouded in fog; he would claim the spot for Spain.

Sebastían Vizcaíno had sailed along the coast of Alta California for Spain in 1692 and found bays that could be defended. British pirates like Francis Drake claimed to have landed somewhere near the area where Anza intended to establish a presidio, a pueblo settlement, and Misíon San Francisco de Asís. Fur hunters sailing south from Russian Alaska had made occasional landfall, braving the coastal fogs to make way toward Spanish land.

In 1769 Spaniard Gaspar de Portolá had reported that his expedition north of Monterey saw an unknown *el brazo del mar,* an arm of the sea. A year before Anza's band set out, Juan Manuel de Ayala explored and charted islands and the coast along a large bay, recording in his journal a "fine harbor [that] presents a beautiful fitness, no lack of good drinking water and plenty of firewood and ballast." These early discoveries described the port of Anza's quest: a harbor where cattle ranchers could ship the hides and tallow they produced that were desperately needed in the rest of Alta California and Mexico.

Anza's soldiers and pioneers left Tubac on October 23, 1775, with pack mules rather than the wagons or carts that would have slowed them down. They stayed in Tucson and then Anza, and the Franciscan padre, Fray Pedro Font, wandered through the ruins at Casa Grande. On the last day of November, Anza's expedition forded the Colorado River after meeting with a Yuma Indian leader. It was winter in the desert, and the water and weather were bitterly cold.

For ten days in December, Anza divided the pioneers into three groups for easier travel. After the expedition regrouped, they heard of the bloody Indian uprising at Misíon San Diego de Alcalá. Anza's party still continued to San Diego Presidio and then made their way north through Alta California, staying at other missions along the way.

Traveling in winter, the valuable cattle had green hillsides to graze and no desert heat to contend with and thus were healthier, allowing the group to move quickly, despite swollen creeks and muddy trails.

On March 10, Anza's group arrived at the Presidio of Monterey and was welcomed the next day by the Alta California mission leader, Fray Junípero Serra. The people and animals rested in the relative luxury of Monterey's settled port.

Anza, Moraga, Fray Font, and a scouting party set off on March 23 to find the harbor that they would name for San Francisco de Asís, the monk from Assisi who loved animals. For seventeen days they surveiled the streams, creeks, lakes, hills, and bay of the future San Francisco settlement.

Anza chose a windy place for the presidio on top of a white cliff, planting a wooden Holy Cross at the point where the entrance to the bay narrowed. His notes and land claims for the Spanish crown were buried at its foot. The explorers noted the constant wind from the northwest and the sand dunes with low-lying bushes and grasses. Fog and frequent cloudy days would make crop cultivation easier than in the desert. The cattle would graze on solid ground among the many marshy areas around the shore.

Pedro Font was enthusiastic about the site for the latest mission but was observant and practical. In his notebook he wrote that the natural port of San Francisco is a "marvel of nature and might well be called a harbor of harbors."

Finally, they returned to Monterey, confident of the new settlement site's natural resources and security against a sea attack. In late April, Anza and Font prepared to return to Tubac and Mexico City to report on the expedition. Moraga was chosen to lead the settlers and cattle from Monterey to their promised land. There was a flurry of activity in Monterey as they made the final arrangements.

Refreshed and stocked with a few weeks' worth of provisions, the colonists set out in June. On June 27, Moraga selected a new presidio site with some shelter from the wind where a fort could defend the ocean entrance to the beautiful bay. Two days later, the priests would celebrate the new settlement's first Mass. Moraga's soldiers were already building a holy arbor of marsh tule reeds for a mission chapel in a sheltered, sunny place on the Laguna de los Dolores. The small creek would give Misíon San Francisco de Asís its familiar name, Mission Dolores.

As Moraga strode between soldiers and settlers, cows mooed. He was the Presidio commandante. He was in charge! But Moraga couldn't know that his soldiers would soon be shivering, naked and cold, and that provisions would be weeks in coming when they finally arrived from Monterey. Supply ships only called once per year. Government budgeting would leave half of Moraga's garrison without lances, swords, pistols, or muskets. In the coming years, visiting ships' crews would steal scarce provisions. The post at the edge of Spain's empire would eke out an existence, virtually ignored by governors, viceroys, and the crown.

But, on June 27, 1776, the settlers were glad to be there, in their new home. Only one soul had been lost en route—in childbirth—and two infants had been born. The colonists were busy looking for trees to build shelter, finding mud to make adobe bricks, and bedding down the cows, horses, and mules. The journey that began as a winter cattle drive in October 1775 at Tubac Presidio had now come to an end.

MARSH TO MISSION

- 1777 -

FRAY FRANCISCO PALÓU CAREFULLY INSCRIBED Chamis's new Christian name, Francisco Moraga, in the new Mission Dolores baptismal register. It was June 24, 1777, San Francisco's mission was less than one year old, and the Franciscan priests in charge had baptized their first local Indian convert to Christianity. Palóu's military counterpart in colonization and conversion of the local residents, Presidio Commandante José Joaquin Moraga, had stood as Chamis's godfather.

Chamis was a Yelamu Ohlone, a twenty-year-old native who lived in a tiny village near the Laguna de los Dolores not far from the mission named for St. Francis of Assisi known as Mission Dolores. The convert's first name honored the founder of the Franciscan religious order, a name that Fray Palóu shared. Chamis's was the first of almost 7,200 baptisms to be recorded through 1845 in the Mission Dolores register, the period when the Franciscans were in charge. Almost 6,700 of the baptized were Native Californians from other Ohlone groups on the southeastern side of San Francisco or the San Francisco Peninsula.

Palóu remembered when Moraga's men had set up camp the prior June that "many pagan Indians appeared in a friendly manner and with expressions of joy at our coming. Their satisfaction increased when they experienced the kindness with which we treated them and when they received the trinkets we would give them in order to attract them." The Ohlones returned and presented shellfish and seeds to the newcomers.

For each mission Palóu and his mentor, Fray Junípero Serra, the father-president of the California missions, were charged by the Spanish king with converting the local Indians. At the same time they were to set up a self-sustaining mission church, dormitories, a cloister, workshops, and outbuildings to function as a miniature village. Agricultural activities, from crops to cattle ranching, aided the self-contained mission community. The mandate was to train natives to succeed them and to secularize each mission by handing it over to the local settlement within ten years.

With the assistance of Presidio soldiers and Moraga's settler families, the padres eagerly celebrated the first Mass a few days after arriving, and by September 1776 there were some permanent buildings ready to formally dedicate in October. As at other missions in Baja California and at the five missions in Alta California that preceded Mission Dolores, the Franciscans patronized the Ohlones as people living, as Palóu assessed it, "in poverty," whose souls needed saving and whose own culture was to be replaced.

Despite the fog and dampness, Ohlone men had been naked and the women had covered their fronts and backs with only reed skirts, the friars noted. Only during very cold weather did both sexes wear capes, usually of rabbit fur. At puberty Ohlone girls received green, black, or blue tattoos on their upper bodies and faces. For ceremonies, the Ohlone used local minerals like cinnabar and various muds that yielded red, yellow, and black body paint. The padres soon clothed the converts—called neophytes—in pants and shirts or long skirts and blouses for the women.

The Spaniards found that the local Ohlone bathed frequently and the men used fire-fueled sweat lodges to keep clean. Fleas were a constant problem on the sandy dunes and marshes between San Francisco's hills, and the Ohlone built small round huts of tule reed brush and matted ferns held up by poles that could easily be burned when fleas got to be too much. For medicine a shaman used herbs, rattles, and the force of voice to heal or deal with demons.

Ohlone villagers worked together to hunt, fish, care for their children, and deal with disputes with other tribes. Battles were not common, as long as one of the small tribes did not invade another's traditional land boundaries, murder, or poach food sources. The Ohlone traded with other native groups to the north and east, even though the language spoken by the tribes in California could be vastly different from village to village.

A hunter would dress like his prey to hunt deer and could bring down a moderately sized tule elk or antelope with a bow and arrows. Grizzly bears and mountain lions roamed the area, and smaller birds—though not the clan-defining eagle, owl, or crow—were hunted or trapped. The Ohlone living near the bay and its extensive marshlands built small boats of tule reeds tied together to make watertight canoes. Nets captured fish, and the women used their fine, hand-woven baskets to gather crabs, clams, and mussels. They also gathered berries, edible flowers, wild grapes, carrots, onions, and roots. Four kinds of oak acorns were stored in animal-thwarting tripod-supported baskets to be ground with mortar and pestle as the staple flour for mush and flat bread.

In contrast with what the natives hunted and gathered, Spaniards introduced corn, beans, and great quantities of wheat. They prepared the wheat mostly as porridge. Bathing was not a priority, and clothing, especially dirty clothing, attracted the ever-present fleas. Epidemics claimed many neophytes who had never developed a resistance to the European diseases. No one took a census, but during the mission period, disease and mistreatment may have reduced California's native population from 72,000 to 18,000.

Neophytes became the unpaid, generally hungry, overworked labor force for the mission fathers. Indian converts built and painted the church and hospital, tended the cattle, milked the dairy cows, made the wine, grew the crops, repaired tools, washed, cleaned, swept, cooked, baked, sewed, and even entertained important mission visitors with colorful dances and costumes that they had left behind upon conversion. French sea explorer, Jean-François de la Pérouse, visited the Monterey Mission in 1786 and reported that the natives, "too much a child, too much a slave, too little a man," were beaten but were expected to understand everything while embracing the Franciscans' God and way of life.

Yet, converts were won over, and in 1783 the permanent Mission Dolores foundation stones would be in place. Indians would manufacture 26,000 adobe building bricks in time for the church's dedication in 1791. Fray Palóu, writing his account of mission history in Mexico City, would remember another detail about his first San Francisco convert. Chamis—Francisco Moraga—had been the first Native Californian to wed at Mission Dolores.

THE TRAGIC ROMANCE OF
CONCHA AND NIKOLAI

- 1806 -

María de la Concepción Marcela Arguello, daughter of the Presidio's commandante, Don José Dario Arguello, expected to be married soon. Everyone said fifteen-year-old María, known as Conchita—or Concha as she preferred—was the most beautiful young woman in the Californias. Because Concha's arranged marriage would cement ties between important families, love was not a consideration, and many men who would inherit ranches someday came in droves to court the young woman.

The Arguello family, though respected and considered well off by local standards, was not from the Spanish aristocracy. Concha, however, loved to read about the larger world and culture at the European royal courts in the moments between dancing masters, sewing lessons, learning to manage a household, and Catholic religious instruction. Occasional visitors shared news of kings, France's Emperor Napoleon, wars, and shifting political alliances between the European powers.

In 1806 the Presidio fort remained the northernmost military outpost for Spain's distant colony in Alta California. Not much had changed since the fort and mission settlement were founded thirty years before. The original Presidio commandante's family, the Moragas, lived near the Arguellos. Franciscan friars stopped by frequently to talk to the women, discuss business with the men, and drink hot chocolate. The local eligible bachelors rode horses, danced with the ladies, ate, drank wine, played cards, and tended to their ranches.

On April 8, 1806, the *Juno* sailed into San Francisco Bay flying a white, blue, and red Russian flag. Spaniards stationed at the outpost of their empire were wary of foreigners. Pirates were always a risk and Russians were known to live in Sitka, Alaska, thousands of miles north on the Pacific Coast. But a Russian ship sailing by the Presidio into the bay was either an act of desperation or a declaration of war.

Commandante Arguello was away in Monterey, so Don Luis, Concha's brother, greeted the Russians. One of the Franciscan padres and the ship's doctor made the introductions in Latin.

Commander of the *Juno,* Nikolai Petrovich Rezanov, an aristocrat and chamberlain to Russian Tsar Alexander I, was on a desperate secret mission. No one was to know that the Russian American Company fur traders in Sitka, Alaska, were starving and needed food and supplies.

Russia had sent a worldly, pleasant representative to San Francisco, an experienced courtier, civil servant, and stockholder in the Russian American Company. Rezanov's approach was not warlike, but polite, and he was determined to be friendly and reassuring. His experience in the Russian court in St. Petersburg included personal commissions for Tsarina Catherine the Great, followed by service in Siberia and trade negotiations with Japan. With little to trade, he needed to plead his case without arousing Spanish fears of a Russian threat. Under no circumstances could he admit that he had to move quickly to get the supplies shipped back north before more Russians died and winter set in.

The Arguellos and the San Francisco community welcomed the cultured forty-two-year-old into their homes and lives. Rezanov pleaded with Alta California's governor and Commandante Arguello to sell him grain and other supplies. The Spaniards refused, fearing punishment for helping an enemy if Spain and Russia were currently at war. No one knew if Rezanov's crew was on a scouting mission to take over the Presidio or to set up a rival Russian settlement close by. Rezanov's charm almost won over the Spanish officials; they were pleased by his intelligence and sophistication but still would not negotiate. Rezanov remained desperate, even as he set up a business office in one room of the Arguello home.

Left a widower with two children in Russia, Rezanov was never one to miss an opportunity. He began to court Concha. Even though she was so young and chaperoned everywhere she went, Concha was fascinated by Rezanov's attention toward her and his tales of life in the imperial Russian court. Nikolai's wealthy first wife had been fifteen when they wed. This bright-eyed girl with white teeth, a lovely smile, and shapely figure was equally eligible.

Nikolai may have used Concha as an excuse to break through the stonewalling as he negotiated, politically insuring a warm Russian reception in California. Though never alone, Concha and Nikolai managed to talk during long walks along the Presidio's bluffs, and when Nikolai proposed marriage, Concha accepted.

New negotiations began, but this time with Concha's parents, who were shocked at the idea of their devout Catholic daughter considering a Russian Orthodox suitor; they considered Rezanov's proposal heresy. Concha pleaded to them that she loved the Russian.

"My proposal shocked her parents, raised in fanaticism," wrote Rezanov in his journal. "The difference in religion and the future separation from their daughter were like a thunderclap to them."

Her sympathetic confessor, one of the Franciscan priests, spoke to the Arguellos. Their priest's persuasion and Rezanov's vows that he would speed back to Russia to secure the assent of his tsar, the Russian Orthodox Church, and the Pope, led to the betrothal of Nikolai and Concha. Concha gave Nikolai a locket with strands of her hair as a betrothal gift. The storehouse was opened, and the *Juno* was loaded for the return voyage to Sitka. Before parting, Nikolai assured Concha, her parents, the priests, and the community that it would take two years or less to get the permissions and dispensations to marry. As Nikolai sailed away on May 21, six weeks after his arrival, Concha stood waving until the sails disappeared. The ship's doctor noted in his journal that, for future trade relations, Rezanov had "decided to sacrifice himself, by wedding Dona Concepción, to the welfare of his country and to bind in friendly alliance Spain and Russia."

Rezanov made it to Sitka with his shipload and then hurried to Russia. Pneumonia and fevers made him delirious. Alone in Siberia on March 1, 1807, halfway home to St. Petersburg, Rezanov fell off his horse and died in the snow.

No one knows when Concha heard the news or whether the locket was returned to her, as legend holds. Concha quickly took orders as a Dominican nun and never again spoke of her love for Nikolai or their tragic romance.

EUREKA! GOLDEN BOOMTOWN

- 1849 -

IT WAS A STORM OF HOPE, LONGING, URGENT DESIRE, and raw greed pushing people to get to California's goldfields in 1849. The Gold Rush began one year after carpenter James Marshall spotted bright pebbles in the American River at Sutter's Mill in Coloma. He had stood in the winter-chilled waters, 45 miles east of Sutter's Fort, on January 14, 1848, wondering if the shine in his palm was really gold. It was.

Marshall's boss, John Augustus Sutter, hoped to keep the news of gold to himself by urging his men to concentrate on the work at hand—building the mill—but with 300 employees, word of the discovery eventually hit California's population center, San Francisco. However, on March 15, the news of the day hardly excited the city's 800 residents when the *Californian* reported a small story on the last page about the discovery of gold at Sutter's Mill. The news from February 2, when Mexico had ceded California to the United States by signing the Treaty of Guadalupe Hidalgo, remained foremost on the people's minds.

Mormon pioneer Sam Brannan owned San Francisco's rival paper, the *California Star;* and he gave the gold find a quick mention. Brannan decided that folks back East might buy the property he was trying to unload in San Francisco if he promoted mining's golden possibilities. He shipped a special edition of the *California Star* to New York and took off to Coloma to see how much gold really existed there.

"Gold! Gold! Gold from the American River," shouted Brannan to San Franciscans when he returned on May 12, 1848. In his fist was a bottle of gold dust. He cared little about the gold, but cared a lot about selling goods and supplies to miners and prospectors.

Even Brannan underestimated the impact of his news. Overnight, any able-bodied man in San Francisco hightailed it to the Sierra Nevada foothills to pan for gold. Prospecting meant wading through cold rivers and streams or standing on the shore in rough pants, a red flannel shirt, boots, and a wide-brimmed hat. San Francisco's population shrunk to less than 200, the school and both newspapers closed, and ships and shops were abandoned.

In the East Coast newspapers, residents began to hear sensational reports of gold finds. The *New York Herald* printed the following in an 1849 special edition:

EL DORADO
OF THE
UNITED STATES OF AMERICA

—

THE DISCOVERY
OF
INEXHAUSTIBLE GOLD MINES
IN
CALIFORNIA

—

Tremendous Excitement among the
Americans

—

The Extensive Preparations
TO
MIGRATE TO THE GOLD REGION
&c, &c, &c.
The great discovery of gold, in dust, scales and lumps,
of quicksilver, platina, cinnabar, &c., &c., on the
shores of the Pacific, has thrown the American people
into a state of wildest excitement. The intelligence from
California, that gold can be picked up in lumps,
weighing six or seven ounces, and scooped up in tin
pans at the rate of a pound of pure dust a scoop, whilst
rich supplies of quicksilver, platina, &c., &c., are so
plentiful as to be entirely neglected for the more pre-
cious metal, has set the inhabitants of this great repub-
lic almost crazy. "Ho! for California," is the cry every
where.

Letters with glowing reports of gold nuggets popping out of the rock started flowing from miners back to relatives in the East. Most did not mention what they called "Seeing the Elephant," the dysentery, scurvy, starvation, and discouragement that most of them faced.

On December 8, 1848, President James K. Polk told the U.S. Congress that the gold reports had been verified. The trickle of gold prospectors turned into a flood.

An estimated 40,000 prospectors and settlers started overland in April 1849, after the snows melted on the California and Santa Fe Trails. The year was wetter than average. The incoming prospectors faced floods, mud, and four to six months of tedious walking or bouncing painfully up and down while driving the oxen that pulled their canvas-covered wagons.

Some 49ers, as the Gold Rush migrants were dubbed, arrived at San Francisco's seaport by ship. Someone named them Argonauts after the Greek myth of Jason and his crew of Argonauts who sought the Golden Fleece. The Argonauts' South America route took six to nine months to sail from New York around Cape Horn to San Francisco. Their timing depended on the ferocity of the winds in the narrow Strait of Magellan. Other prospectors took a ship to Mexico or Nicaragua, trekked west, and then headed north to San Francisco. Sixty years before the Panama Canal, the fastest journey was via ship to Panama, then overland through insect-ridden jungles to the Pacific where a fast steamer ship then headed for San Francisco.

The discovery of gold drew immigrants from around the world. Coal miners came from Cornwall, and skilled miners arrived from Mexico and Chile. The riots of 1848 and revolutions in France, Germany, and Italy made political refuge in a rich new land attractive. But in the mining camps, the Native Americans and Chinese were treated as servants or like slaves.

One out of five gold miners died in the Gold Rush's first year. Those who survived a season or two in the gold mining camps jumped at a chance to escape to the lantern-lit city. But they would soon find out that San Francisco was expensive; its currency was gold—nuggets or dust. A dozen eggs cost $10. In 1849 it was cheaper to send laundry to China than to have it done locally. Ironically, the pricey settlement's streets weren't paved and the harbor had no wharf to offload passengers, goods, and supplies. Sanitation was nonexistent; sand fleas and rats plagued the streets.

The saloons, taverns, gambling dens, brothels, bakeries, and wooden boardinghouses readily met the human tide streaming back from the goldfields in search of good food, whiskey, entertainment, and success in life. The lively town that was smelly, dusty, dirty, and strewn with trash nonetheless began to fill up with doctors, lawyers, farmers, bankers, shopkeepers, and laborers.

Some 49ers would return to their original homes, with little gold to show for their efforts. Some moved on to 1850s gold rushes in Australia, New Zealand, and British Columbia, Canada. And some 49ers decided to stay in San Francisco where they set up businesses to serve the needs of new arrivals.

By 1850, when gold insured California's admission into the United States, San Francisco's population had swollen to 25,000. The backwater that had become an overnight boomtown was starting to settle down. But San Francisco would never lose its reputation as a slightly naughty, forward-minded spot where an enterprising new arrival could prosper.

BLUE JEANS

- 1853 -

NEWLY MINTED AMERICAN CITIZEN LEVI STRAUSS walked off the Pacific Mail Steamer *Isthmus* onto San Francisco's docks on March 14, 1853, amid a sea of abandoned ships' masts. The desolate, creaking wooden hulls, some half-submerged in the San Francisco Bay and most without any nails or remaining metal fixtures, could have been a very bad sign.

For the son of a Jewish peddler who had been born in Bavaria, north of Nuremberg, Germany, the deserted ships and the busy bayside implied just the opposite—opportunity. Captains, sailors, crewmen, and ship passengers had raced to San Francisco during the Gold Rush several years before. Most had never looked back in the dash to prospect for gold in the Sierra Nevada. Men like twenty-four-year-old Strauss—who had changed his birth name, Loeb, to a name easier to pronounce when he arrived in New York City in 1847—intended to supply the gold prospectors and everyone else who needed clothing and dry goods, at a fine profit over New York prices.

Strauss's half-brothers had started a wholesale dry goods business in New York in 1848. Levi received on-the-job training there before briefly heading west to peddle his half-brothers' cloth and clothing in Kentucky.

Then, Gold Rush fever struck America. Levi Strauss eventually followed his sister and brother-in-law to California along with hundreds of thousands of gold prospectors. First, though, he returned to New York to pack a stock of goods to sell when he arrived in the West. In February 1853, Levi eagerly boarded a sailing ship to Panama and later caught the steamer *Isthmus* to the Promised Land.

Strauss and his brother-in-law, David Stern, could have gone down in history as merely anonymous wholesale dry goods entrepreneurs in a lively booming city. But together they created a powerful partnership as businessmen and wholesalers. The partners slept in their warehouse to meet ships and get the best prices for auctioned cargos. Strauss had learned that a smart businessman paid attention to the ultimate consumer, and that a smart wholesaler would search for products to sell to a retailer who, in turn, would sell the target consumer something the customer wanted or needed.

Prospectors and other manual laborers needed pants that were sturdy with pockets that didn't rip out when dirt, gold nuggets, coins, currency, tools, and watches were crammed inside. Pants, the trousers of the era, were often thin, prone to tearing, and flimsy—problematic for men whose seat wore through or whose knees went threadbare. Decades later legend would have it that Levi Strauss was inspired by the durability of Conestoga wagon canvas. He envisioned a thick but rugged pair of what he called "waist-high overalls" tailored out of canvas, something a desperate miner would pay for with gold dust.

If there was any record of the invention of denim jeans known as Levi's, it was lost in the 1906 Earthquake. What is certain is that

Strauss's half brothers provided the strong blue cotton denim cloth that he contracted tailors to sew into waist-high overalls. Merchants found that Strauss's pants lasted much longer, but the pockets still gave way.

While the wholesale business flourished, Levi lived with his sister and brother-in-law and his nephews. By 1866 he could lavishly spend $25,000 on gaslight chandeliers and a new-fangled freight elevator for Levi Strauss and Co. headquarters. A lifelong bachelor, Strauss gave money to charities to help orphans, establish schools, and support the activities of his synagogue.

Unlike many of his competitors, Strauss was willing to extend credit to even marginal suppliers like his contract tailors. One of the tailors on Levi Strauss's lists in 1870 was Jacob Davis, a Jewish immigrant from Russia living in Reno, Nevada. Davis sewed a heavy-duty pair of pants for a woodcutter, using copper rivets at the corners of the front and back pockets, much as he had done to prevent corners of horse blankets from unraveling. Miners and others who saw satisfied customers wearing Davis's rivet pants knew that someone had solved pocket gouging. Davis was overwhelmed with orders for 200 pairs of his rivet pants in eighteen months. Due to the high demand Davis could not fulfill all the orders that were coming in, and he did not have the $68 it cost to file for a patent on his pocket rivet process.

Davis appealed to fellow pant producer and source of credit, Levi Strauss, to file for the patent in his name and offered to split the profits. In 1872 Strauss filed jointly for his company and Davis's patent process. Patent number 139,121 was issued to them on May 20, 1873, a month after Davis had willingly sold his share to Strauss and moved to San Francisco to supervise production of the waist-high overalls with pocket rivets and orange seam thread. From June through December 1873, in the midst of a national economic depression, Levi Strauss and Co. sold $43,510 in riveted denim pants.

The wholesaler dived into production with a Fremont Street factory. With production no longer outsourced to many home-based tailors, everything was produced in the new factory out of denim or duck canvas by a Chinese cloth cutter and sixty white seamstresses. Each woman earned a wage equivalent to a skilled laborer sewing entire pairs of pants, rather than repetitively sewing only parts of the whole. Italian, Irish, and Spanish women worked together and called the boss "Levi," not Mr. Strauss.

Salesmen fanned out worldwide, offering waist-high overalls and full-body overalls to both men and women, with the pitch, "These goods are specially adapted for the use of farmers, mechanics, miners and working men in general." Strauss backed his pants with a free replacement guarantee.

In 1880 the company sold $2.4 million of Levi's pants, and in 1890, when Levi and his four nephews incorporated the company, the waist-high overall pants were given the lot number name, 501R, a legacy that remains in the trademarked 501 jeans.

Levi Strauss died in 1902, leaving $6 million to his nephews and charities. He never did call his durable pants "jeans." But jeans became a symbol of the West and the fashion statement of cowboys, movie stars, models, and 1960s counterculture.

JUSTICE AT FORT GUNNYBAGS

- 1856 -

WARNING!

NOTICE IS GIVEN that any person found
Pilfering, Stealing, Robbing, or committing
any act of Lawless Violence will be summarily
HANGED

—Vigilance Committee

THE RESTLESS MOB OF 20,000, half the residents of San Francisco, had gotten wind of an execution—or maybe a double hanging—and had rushed downtown. San Francisco's second Committee of Vigilance in five years was about to apply frontier justice to two men for first-degree murder.

Sweaty bodies filled Sacramento Street between Battery and Davis Streets with an eerie silence. Fear and curiosity aroused a strange satisfaction among the people—a weeks-long battle between tabloid newspaper publishers that had ended in murder was coming to an end. A 6-foot-thick barrier of rough, sand-filled gunnysacks stood 10 feet high at the entrance to the committee's headquarters. Cannons faced the crowd from the building's corners. According to rumor there were 3,500 muskets ready to take on anyone who dared attack the committee. One way or another, the Committee of Vigilance would take action or be eliminated by troops organized by the Law and Order Party, led by San Francisco's corrupt sheriff.

Earlier that day, May 22, 1856, the newspaper publisher of the evening *San Francisco Bulletin,* James King of William, had died of gunshot wounds. On May 14, James P. Casey, city supervisor and editor of the *San Francisco Sunday Times,* had drawn a large revolver and shot King in the street in broad daylight. King, who had made a fortune as a banker after the Gold Rush and lost it all before starting the *Bulletin,* had railed against corruption in government. Like many others, Casey had stuffed the ballot box to get elected. King discovered that Casey had once been an inmate of New York's infamous Sing Sing penitentiary. When his prison history was published in one of King's many muckraking editorials, Casey took revenge.

King did not die that day and lingered on for a week. Casey knew the 1851 Committee of Vigilance had concluded that unscrupulous Gold Rush-era arrivals and ex-convicts from Australia called "Sydney Ducks" were responsible for crimes and fires that burned the wooden settlement down several times and that many of that committee's members were ready to exact justice again. The first committee had arrested ninety, hung four, whipped one man, deported twenty-eight, and handed fifteen over to the law for court trials.

Since then San Francisco's crime rate had not improved. An 1855 survey found that there had been 1,200 murders in four years. Between 1849 and 1856, more than 1,000 homicides went unpunished. Politicians were corrupt, and law enforcement officials were often in cahoots with the criminals. Mayors and California's governors did what they could, but it was not enough. The man who had taken command of the militia guarding San Francisco just a few days before King's assassination, General William Tecumseh Sherman, recalled,

> *Politics had become a regular and profitable business,*
> *and politicians were more than suspected of being cor-*
> *rupt. It was reported and currently believed that the*
> *sheriff (Scannell) had been required to pay the Democ-*
> *ratic Central Committee a hundred thousand dollars*
> *for his nomination, which was equivalent to an elec-*
> *tion, for an office of the nominal salary of twelve thou-*
> *sand dollars a year for four years.*

After King's shooting, Casey turned himself in to Scannell to be locked up in jail so Casey's politically influential friends would be assured of his safety and King's supporters would know he had not fled. In the week that followed, as King lingered near death, Sherman and California Governor John Neely Johnson tried to get the U.S. Army and Navy involved in civilian policing of San Francisco. The army general dithered and Commodore David Farragut, later the Navy's first admiral during the Civil War, offered only a sloop in the bay for moral effect.

Governor Johnson pleaded with his good friend, William Coleman, who was the head of the Committee of Vigilance, to punish Casey. After King died, Johnson asked for a grand jury to indict Casey and asked a well-respected judge to try him speedily. The governor would personally guarantee that Casey would be tried. Coleman said Sheriff Scannell colluded with dirty politicians and violated the public trust, but that he would talk to the committee. Enraged at

Governor Johnson's negotiation with the Vigilantes, Scannell's Law and Order group formed a posse.

When King died, General Sherman and Governor Johnson watched armed crowds marching to the jail on Broadway. Soon Casey emerged, quickly followed by another prisoner, Charles Cora. Cora was awaiting retrial for the November 1855 murder of a U.S. Marshall who had publicly insulted Cora's mistress, Belle, at a local theatre. The hung jury had sympathized with Cora's motive of love as his defense.

Casey and Cora were loaded into a carriage, and the gathering crowd followed to the Committee of Vigilance building on Sacramento Street. The accused murderers went inside the fortified building to face 3,500 armed Vigilantes now assembled to mete out justice. The news of a quick trial and its consequences spread through San Francisco. The crowd swelled. Inside, each man had an attorney, but the committee verdict was swift: death by execution.

The Vigilantes quickly suspended two 3-square-foot wooden platforms from the second-story roof of Fort Gunnybags. The assembled citizens, who were kept 100 yards from the fortified building, caught a collective breath, and the air grew still. At 1:15 P.M. two men with bound elbows appeared. Nooses were put around their necks. Cora, with his head wrapped with a white cloth, stood silent. Casey's noose was briefly removed as he spoke to a priest. He told the crowd, *"Gentlemen, Fellow Citizens—I am not guilty of any crime."*

Casey pleaded with the newspapers not to persecute his memory, hoping his mother would never hear of the murder charge. He cried out that he had never meant to commit murder.

As *Town Talk* reported, both men were "launched into eternity." One hour elapsed before the coroner claimed the swinging bodies of Casey and Cora.

A month later, on June 21, California Supreme Court Judge David S. Terry, a Law and Order Party man, stabbed a Committee of Vigilance policeman in the neck with a Bowie knife. The Vigilantes took Terry into custody, but he managed to escape to Farragut's naval sloop. Others were tried and executed by the Committee of Vigilance before the group disbanded quietly in August. Years later, General Sherman reflected on those days:

> *As they controlled the press, they wrote their own history, and the world generally gives them the credit of having purged San Francisco of its rowdies and roughs; but their success has given great stimulus to a dangerous principle, that would at any time justify the mob in seizing all power of government; and who is to say that the Vigilance committee may not be composed of the worst, instead of the best, elements of a community? Indeed, in San Francisco, as soon as it was demonstrated that the real power had passed from the City Hall to the committee-room, the same set of bailiffs, constables, and rowdies that had infested City Hall were found in the employment of the "Vigilantes;"* . . .

FIRE LADY

- 1858 -

ONE AFTERNOON IN 1858, THE VOLUNTEER FIREFIGHTERS of Knicker-bocker Engine Company No. 5 were struggling against time. Up the nearly vertical Telegraph Hill they pulled their fire engine. In those days when a slope was too steep for horses, the strong men pulled the engine and water tank to the scene of a fire. The volunteer fire "boys," as people fondly called them, were summoned from their usual jobs by an alarm bell. Donning their red shirts and protective hats with back brims, they raced to their engine's ropes.

A few minutes could make all the difference. Sweat dripped from their foreheads beneath their leather fireman caps. Hauling uphill was slow. People in the street could hear engine wheels creaking up the hill and the firemen's heavy breathing.

Manhattan Engine No. 2 and Howard Engine No. 3 had proba-bly heard the alarm, too, and gathered their volunteers for the haul up the hill. Each company saw the arrival of another engine company first at the scene as an insult to its pride, preparedness, and strength. Knickerbocker No. 5 simply had to be first.

On their way up the hill, the Knickerbocker volunteers vaguely heard the thud of books being tossed on the ground by nearby schoolgirls. A whirl of skirts flew at them and a pretty little girl picked up one of the hauling ropes yelling, "Come on, you men! Everybody pull and we'll beat 'em!" By this point the men had already hauled their engine nearly one mile.

The men remembered that other bystanders had rushed to help after the little girl's cries. They found out later that the fifteen-year-old girl's name was Lillie. Lillie Hitchcock's family had moved to San Francisco in 1851 when she was eight years old. In her childhood, fires were an ever-present threat.

In less than a decade since the Gold Rush had brought thousands of settlers, San Francisco had had a horrid history of fires. Between December 24, 1849, and June 22, 1851, six fires had burned most of the wooden buildings in the city to the ground. Because homes, storefronts, and warehouse districts were built so close together, all the structures became engulfed in flames. Residents would set up camp in the parks or stay with friends until their houses were rebuilt, usually within a few weeks.

Lillie Hitchcock's family was never sure why Lillie was so alert every time the fire alarm bell rang out. Her father, Dr. Charles M. Hitchcock, had been a physician at West Point when Elizabeth ("Lillie") Wyche Hitchcock was born in 1842. Her mother tried to raise Lillie in the upper-class society her Virginia family was accustomed to.

But Lillie was crazy about firefighters and their work. There was no stopping her after she had inspired the Knickerbocker Engine crew. She raced to the aid of Engine No. 5 with every alarm. The men were amused and proud of the petite girl's bravery. Lillie once said that she loved courage in a uniform; her remark was widely repeated around town.

Knickerbocker Engine Company No. 5 had become one of thirteen volunteer squads loosely organized as the San Francisco Fire Department. There was also three specialized hook-and-ladder companies responsible for reaching fires raging on higher floors and sending water into the blaze from above.

Being a volunteer firefighter was a rich man's activity. The time spent together during drills was not only about practicing with water, hoses, and buckets, but also a kind of men's club for business and political networking. However, the "club" was serious enough to impose a fine on a member if he missed a mandatory meeting or a fire.

The companies followed a volunteer system based on the first fire brigade that Benjamin Franklin founded in Philadelphia in 1736. Men in a community paid for the privilege to join a brigade or fire company. They also paid for their own uniforms, equipment, furniture from the finest woods, books for their libraries, entertainment, and the company engine itself. In the 1850s, a shiny engine cost $3,000–5,000. The completely furnished firehouse for the Sansome Hook and Ladder Company No. 3 cost a princely $44,000. Knickerbocker Engine Company No. 5 was organized in October 1850, and by 1853 had paid $8,000 for its second firehouse plus $2,000 for furnishings.

Lillie became the Knickerbocker's mascot, and on October 3, 1863, the men elected her an honorary member of the company. They gave her a fireman's red shirt, a leather firefighter helmet, and a gold badge with the No. 5 company emblem. Lillie proudly wore that badge everywhere she went for the rest of her life. San Franciscans cheered whenever she appeared in parades atop a fire engine.

When she married a stock exchange trader, Benjamin Coit, and became Mrs. Lillie Hitchcock-Coit, every bed sheet, piece of linen, handkerchief, and blouse in her house had the No. 5 insignia. By that time she had stopped chasing fire engines, but sent gifts each year for the company's annual banquet, visited sick Knickerbockers in the hospitals, and sent flowers to their funerals.

Even after she moved away to live and travel in Europe, San Franciscans never forgot the plucky girl. She returned from Paris several times, scandalizing San Francisco again by living as she wished—drinking whiskey, smoking, and playing poker. Lillie always visited *her* firefighters, who by 1866 were paid professionals and no longer volunteers. When she died in 1929, the eighty-seven-year-old beloved Fire Belle left $5,000 to each surviving member of Knickerbocker No. 5. Another $50,000 bequest was for an artistic sculpture in memory of the original volunteer fire department. And San Francisco received money from her will for "adding to the beauty of the city which I have always loved."

Lillie's legacy, the 180-foot-high Lillie Hitchcock Coit Tower shaped like a fire hose nozzle standing on end, opened in 1933. It stands atop Telegraph Hill. Over to the west, in Washington Square, sits a statue of two volunteer firemen heroically carrying a woman from a fire.

HALLIDIE'S HILL CLIMBER

- 1873 -

SAN FRANCISCO'S TYPICAL SUMMER FOG hovered low in the streets just as it was getting light. On this day, August 2, 1873, inventor and industrial designer Andrew S. Hallidie was ready to test out his latest and most risky invention. A few people were about in the drizzle, curious to see if Hallidie's horseless carriages that he called cable cars could defy gravity on a hill.

Hallidie had hired a gripman to operate the contraption on its inaugural ride along the 307-foot long, 20 percent grade of Clay Street between Jones and Kearny Streets. The gripman was to grab and pull a long, upright handle in the middle of the car, called the grip, that connected to a continuously moving cable beneath the street. Hallidie said the action would move the car forward. To stop, Hallidie instructed the gripman to release the grip.

What the gripman, trained as a locomotive engineer, hadn't counted on was that Hallidie intended to face the car apparatus *down* the hill. The pull of gravity would add to the gripman's challenges. Another challenge was the two-part cable car. The sixteen-passenger traction car with the grip was called a "dummy," while a fourteen-passenger car connected to it was the "trailer."

Hallidie was under pressure. San Francisco supervisors had granted him a permit to try out his "Wire Rope Street Railway," as he called it, by August 1. It was now August 2, and having missed the legal deadline, Hallidie was desperate to succeed. Later, Hallidie would claim that the feat was accomplished on August 1.

Scotsman Andrew Smith Hallidie had arrived in San Francisco in 1852, twenty-one years earlier. The Gold Rush was in high gear and Hallidie used metal wire rope technology that his father had already patented in Scotland to make wire rope for suspension bridges and for Northern California mining operations. As he traveled, surveyed, and built bridges, Hallidie discovered a need for a continually moving pulley. He fine-tuned a metal cable ropeway to haul equipment in California's mines. Hallidie was granted a patent for an "endless cable ropeway" in 1867.

Two years later, Hallidie was standing at the corner of Kearny and Jackson Streets. The city was noisy with passenger carriages, trams clattering over cobblestones, and whinnying horses pulling wagons with heavy loads of supplies to stores and businesses.

As he watched the bustle of traffic, Hallidie heard something and glanced west up the Jackson Street Hill. Sounds of clattering and crashing wood mixed with the terrified neighs of horses falling backward. The wagon, pulled by a five-horse team, was too heavy to make it up the slope. The horses lost their balance and became trapped in the rigging.

The horrifying event that Hallidie witnessed was not uncommon on San Francisco's hills. Supplies were damaged or destroyed, and in the worst-case scenarios, horses and people were injured or killed.

Tram horses were lucky to survive four years. A shocked but observant Hallidie believed he could come up with a solution.

San Francisco attorney Benjamin H. Brooks was already working on a cable railway to solve the hill transport problem. Along with some partners and an engineer, he obtained a cable line franchise in 1870 that would allow a line to extend west several miles from downtown San Francisco. The partners were unable to secure financing, so Brooks, barely able to spare time from a successful law practice, and his team eventually sold the franchise rights to Hallidie.

Hallidie spent the next years and more than $60,000 constructing what local papers called "Hallidie's Folly." He chose the steep, six-block-long Clay Street Hill for his testing ground. Two 150-horsepower steam engines fueled by coal in a nearby powerhouse would move the 11,000 feet of underground wire cable along the Clay Street Hill.

Hallidie waited for the gripman to mount the dummy car. But, the gripman was staring down narrow, 49-foot-wide Clay Street to Portsmouth Square, six steep blocks below. The crowd knew something was wrong. The cable car should be on its way by now if it was going to move at all. This test would prove whether Hallidie had built a runaway mechanical hazard, or, if he was as good a designer as he claimed, a cable car that might make life easier and safer. If he didn't act soon, the day's regular traffic would start making its way up the hill.

Hallidie leaped to the grip as the gripman turned his back and left the scene. If the cable car had been a horse, Hallidie would have seized the reins since it could be considered equivalent to a mechanical horse. The cable car was under control! Hallidie gripped and released as he inched the double-car conveyance forward, down to the first intersection at Mason Street. The cable car leveled out, as it would do at every street crossing to come.

Hallidie had proven the cable car's worth. Immediately the Clay Street Hill Railroad began carrying passengers, including the mayor, up and down the hill. The Clay Street line would be extended west to Van Ness Avenue in 1877. Hallidie became wealthy from the 5-cent fares.

More cable railway lines would be constructed, including one up the California Street Hill by the rich residents of Nob Hill. In 1882 all cable cars added bells to warn pedestrians and horses. Turntables were installed for the major lines to turn cars around 180 degrees so that a car need only go in one direction. By 1900, cable cars were operating in twenty-eight American cities.

But the cable cars' San Francisco heyday, with nine companies operating 600 cars over twenty-two lines, lasted barely three decades. Cheaper electric streetcars with overhead wires were introduced in 1892 and became the city's choice for rebuilding transportation systems after the 1906 Earthquake and Fire. Most cable-car lines, including Hallidie's, were abandoned.

In 1947, Mayor Roger Lapham told San Francisco supervisors, "The city should get rid of its cable cars as soon as possible." Friedel Klussmann, known as the Cable Car Lady, rallied women's and civic groups to save the quaint cable cars as a tourist draw, and voters agreed. In 1964, San Francisco's Cable Cars became a moving National Historic Landmark.

NABOBS OF NOB HILL AND
THE SPITE FENCE

- 1877 -

ALL OF SAN FRANCISCO WAS ABUZZ. Sheer spite, that's what it was. Atop Nob Hill, Charles Crocker's workmen were building a 40-foot-high wooden fence around three sides of the tiny house next door to Crocker's mansion. No one was sure why Crocker, one of the Big Four that had built the mighty Central Pacific Railroad connecting both coasts of the United States, was acting high and mighty, but the gossips were having a field day.

People were calling Crocker's barricade the Spite Fence. An undertaker named Nicolas Yung owned a modest house on the same block as Crocker's mansion at Taylor and California Streets. Yung was the only person who had refused to sell the land his house was built on to Crocker. Crocker wanted to own the whole lot and was determined to get his way. So, he built the Spite Fence hoping that Yung would be so uncomfortable and isolated by the fence that he would sell his land to Crocker and leave.

On May 10, 1869, the Transcontinental Railroad's last spike was driven in the connecting rails at Promontory, Utah, assuring the fortunes of the "Big Four." Crocker, Stanford, Huntington, and Hopkins were California's four railroad tycoons and among the richest men in the state. Leland Stanford, who later became a California governor and founder of Stanford University in his son's memory, was the front man. Collis P. Huntington was the railroad's canny and brainy lobbyist who originally partnered with Mark Hopkins as co-owner of a successful Sacramento general store. Hopkins's attention to bookkeeping, detail, and legalities formed the basis for Charles Crocker's secure financing and organization of Chinese laborers to build the railroad. The profit from rail freight and passenger traffic set the four men up for life.

All of the Big Four eventually built Nob Hill mansions once Andrew Hallidie's Clay Street cable cars made access to the California Street Hill (only two blocks away) possible. By 1878 the California Street cable car was in operation where horse carriages or horse-drawn streetcars previously had been unable to make the steep grade.

The West Coast railroad tycoons, envious of the grandeur of East Coast mansions, were determined to make their statement of success in San Francisco. Unlike New York and other eastern cities with flat-land neighborhoods of mansions, this city had hills to build palaces upon. Standing on the California Street Hill, a San Franciscan could look east toward the banks and bustling business district, north to the sea of ship masts along the wharves and beyond to the mouth of the Sacramento River and Delta, and south to San Mateo.

People started calling the rise 338 feet above sea level Nob Hill. Snob Hill, said the envious. Others claimed that nob was short for *nabob,* a title for Indian Mogul Empire governors. Wags, people who liked to joke, talked about a hill-like bump on the land as a knob, downplaying the hill's height. However it got its name, Nob Hill in the 1870s was becoming the best address in town.

Kentucky-born lawyer turned businessman, James Ben Ali Haggin, who had made a mining fortune with George Hearst, started the Nob Hill land rush. His lavish sixty-one-room house with three conservatories was also renowned for the property's forty-horse stable and eighteen carriages that indulged his passion for horse breeding and racing.

A few millionaires had already built mansions on Nob Hill, but Leland Stanford was the first of the Big Four to tackle a palatial Nob Hill home. The same Rocklin, California, quarry stone used for Central Pacific bridges and tunnels built the retaining wall at California and Powell Streets above which Stanford built his $2-million mansion in 1876. The exterior was California redwood. Inside, a three-story rotunda was topped by stained glass. To further show off their wealth, Stanford and his wife had an art gallery.

Next door, Mark Hopkins's wife, Mary, took charge of overseeing construction of their $3-million mansion that most folks called Hopkins's Castle. Multiple turrets were covered in shingles arranged in patterns. Cupolas were everywhere. The Victorian-era hodgepodge of exterior styles, although constructed of wood, was painted to look like stone. Mark Hopkins had little interest in the project and never lived in the mansion before he died in a railroad car in 1878. Mary Hopkins's mania for any and all embellishments inside the castle's interior resulted in what locals called "eclectic." After Hopkins's death she became even more frivolous by duplicating her building frenzy in Great Barrington, Massachusetts, in the Berkshires. She married the Hopkins's Castle architect who had put up with all her whims.

Huntington chose the center block of Nob Hill and bought the Colton house. David Colton had been the Big Four's chief attorney for the railroad project and was often considered another partner. Colton's white, two-story Italianate house was plainer than most, but because it had so many friezes, columns, and details, most people called it the "wedding cake." A domed, 24-foot ceiling covered a combination music room and art gallery.

In 1877 Charles Crocker started building on the block north of Huntington's Wedding Cake. No one was going to have a larger mansion, more gables, or extravagant towers; his art gallery alone would hold paintings worth more than $1 million. Rivaling or surpassing Mary Hopkins's instinct for embellishment, Crocker, a huge space-dominating man with a double goatee beard, was determined to spare no expense. Just as he had driven Chinese workers to lay a record-breaking 10 miles of railroad track between dawn and sunset when he acted as the Central Pacific's contractor, he would not tolerate anyone who interfered with his plans.

Yung would not sell. Noise of sawing and hammering filled Nob Hill. Crocker's fence went up. Soon only Yung's smoking chimneys were evidence that Yung was living in a small home behind Crocker's huge manse.

Times were tense in the city below in 1877. Loud and outspoken Irish immigrant and labor organizer, Dennis Kearney, stood for immigrant waterfront workers against Chinese workers. He corralled members of the Workingman's Association and marched up Nob Hill to protest Crocker's use of Chinese laborers on the waterfront. Although Yung was never reported to have asked for Kearney's support, Kearney demanded that Crocker remove the fence. Crocker ignored Kearney's appeal, and the workers assembled on Nob Hill.

With delight, San Franciscans heard the tale—never proven false—that shortly after the Spite Fence went up, Yung placed a huge coffin on his roof. The coffin's message was clear: Yung had painted a skull and crossbones on the lid so Crocker could not fail to see it daily as he glared at his neighbor's offending house.

After Yung's death, Yung's heirs sold his patch of land and tiny house to Crocker. Neither Crocker's Mansion nor Yung's house lasted long. The Big Four mansions on Nob Hill all burned to the ground in the 1906 Earthquake and Fire.

LE ROI EST MORT (THE KING IS DEAD)

- 1880 -

"On the reeking pavement, in the darkness of a moon-less night under the dripping rain, and surrounded by a hastily gathered crowd of wondering strangers, Nor-ton I, by the grace of God, Emperor of the United States and Protector of Mexico, departed this life."

—*SAN FRANCISCO CHRONICLE,*
JANUARY 9, 1880

THE BEWHISKERED, SLIGHTLY PUDGY MAN in the formal military uniform sporting a top hat with a plume collapsed in the darkness at California and Dupont Streets. He usually carried a sheathed sword at his hip, but he had left it at his lodging house at Sacramento Street. On his way to a lecture he stopped at the Academy of Natural Sciences, where he fell, causing his umbrella walking stick to clatter to the ground.

Passersby saw Joshua Norton fall and instantly rushed to the aid of His Majesty, the name given to the eccentric character about town by the locals. The policeman who summoned the help required to race the unconscious man through the rain and to the hospital recognized Emperor Norton immediately. But it was too late. The self-proclaimed Emperor of the United States was pronounced dead on arrival.

Norton's imperial proclamations had confounded, amused, and pricked the consciences of San Franciscans since September 17, 1859, the day that he had declared himself emperor. People speculated that he was crazy, a con man, or a little of both. Whatever most citizens privately thought of the man who died in the rain on January 8, the San *Francisco Chronicle* proclaimed public sentiment in the January 11 headline describing his funeral:

LE ROI EST MORT

No one doubted "The King Is Dead." It was one of few facts known about Norton. Joshua Abraham Norton, son of John Norton, died "Aged About 65," the *Chronicle* hedged at the end of its report. Joshua was born in England and had probably lived in South Africa. In 1848 or perhaps late in 1849, he arrived in San Francisco by ship. Unlike other men hoping for Gold Rush luck, it was widely believed that Norton had arrived with $40,000 in cash, likely inherited from his father.

For a few years Norton did well, using his business acumen and contacts as a broker for ships' cargoes. He invested in valuable real estate at Sansome and Jackson Streets by the banks and customs house. People knew him by sight.

But Norton miscalculated. In 1852 he put all of his money on the line to buy a shipload of rice, speculating that cornering the market on the rice supply would make him even richer. He was counting on the Chinese and other Asians in California who ate rice as a staple to buy up the cargo. Suddenly a Japanese ship loaded with rice—cheaper rice—was docked in San Francisco. As a result no one would buy his shipload. He was ruined.

Norton disappeared after his misfortune. Meanwhile, San Francisco was living through the Gold Rush aftermath with the law in the hands of Vigilance committees. The waterfront expanded as the harbor to the east was being filled in with the English ballast stones brought by the clipper ships and the rotting ships themselves. More homes were being built, and culture was moving from dance halls to parlors and opera houses. In 1853 California's Academy of Sciences was founded.

On September 17, 1859, a man in military uniform walked into the editor's office of the *San Francisco Call* and presented a letter that read:

At the peremptory request of a large majority of the citizens of these United States, I, Joshua Norton, formerly of Algoa Bay, Cape of Good Hope, and now for the past nine years and ten months of San Francisco, California, declare and proclaim myself Emperor of these U.S., and in virtue of the authority thereby in me vested, do hereby order and direct the representatives of the different States of the Union to assemble in the Musical Hall of this city on the 1st day of February next, then and there to make such alterations in the existing laws of the Union as may ameliorate the evils under which the country is laboring, and thereby cause confidence to exist, both at home and abroad, in our stability and integrity.

Norton's reappearance and manifesto was on the front page the next morning. From then on, newspaper editors tucked tongues in cheeks and routinely published Emperor Norton's proclamations along with reports of his travels about town. Even if Norton's uniform was shabby and his eyes did not always stare in the same direction, one could count on his grandiose pronouncements. San Francisco loved entertainment, and Norton's spectacle was harmless, peaceful, and filled with amusing rants and outlandish ideas.

Within a month, as support for universal suffrage, Norton decreed the abolition of the United States Congress as a fraudulent and corrupt body. The next year he dissolved the republic in favor of his absolute monarchy. As the Civil War began, he offered President Abraham Lincoln his advice, which Lincoln declined. By 1862 Emperor Norton had added Protector of Mexico to his titles. San Franciscans laughed over their morning papers when his proposal to the widowed Queen Victoria was reported.

Norton persuaded printers to print his money and local merchants to honor it as if it was real. His reputation led printers, hotel owners, restauranteurs, and saloonkeepers to put his charges on the house, often in exchange for a sign in the window that the business was an exclusive purveyor to His Majesty.

For a time two mongrel dogs, Bummer and Lazarus, followed Norton on his rounds around town, eating and drinking where he stopped. They became celebrities. As a reporter for *The Californian* in 1865, it fell to Mark Twain to write in an obituary, "The old vagrant 'Bummer' is really dead at last . . . he dies full of years, and honor, and disease, and fleas."

No one really knew if Norton's freeloading was the act of a man too lazy or too crazy to earn his own money. In 1867 a policeman had the temerity to arrest the Emperor with the intention to send him to a lunatic asylum. An outraged public vented its wrath upon the officer.

Norton was always good for a chuckle. He proclaimed that a suspension bridge should be built from Oakland to San Francisco, to Marin County, and out to offshore islands, then later modifying the plan to have the bridge go over Telegraph Hill to the wharves. To even think about suspending a bridge so far over San Francisco Bay was foolishness in those days. The league of nations Norton proposed may have been considered another one of his hallucinations. People scoffed at most of Norton's ideas, but they did agree with his 1872 proclamation about their city's name:

> *Whoever after due and proper warning shall be heard*
> *to utter the abominable word "Frisco," which has no*
> *linguistic or other warrant, shall be deemed guilty of a*
> *High Misdemeanor, and shall pay into the Imperial*
> *Treasury as penalty the sum of twenty-five dollars.*

When he died, Norton's imperial fortune consisted of five or six dollars in his pockets. The funeral of "a man of imaginary majesty," as the *Chronicle* delicately put it, was not that of a pauper, but that of a sovereign. Between 10,000 and 30,000 mourners—or subjects—followed Norton's coffin to a grave at the Masonic Cemetery. The superstitious speculated that the Emperor had something to do with the full solar eclipse the day after his funeral.

Not all of Norton's proclamations had been bogus. Within forty years of his death, a League of Nations was formed. The United Nations Charter was signed in San Francisco in 1945. The Golden Gate Bridge was suspended over the entrance to the bay in 1937. In 2005 San Francisco supervisors approved a resolution that asked the state to rename the 1936 San Francisco-Oakland Bay Bridge as the Emperor Norton Bridge. And most San Franciscans still won't call their city "Frisco."

CLIFFS, BATHS, AND HEIGHTS

- 1881 -

As HIS FANCY HORSE-DRAWN BUGGY BOUNCED over the sandy road, Adolph Sutro was deep in thought. The millionaire had asked his grown daughter, Emma, for her company on the ride to the seaside. Emma, the eldest of Sutro's six children, always enjoyed being with her serious father. Today he was uncharacteristically quiet.

They were already several miles from downtown, surrounded by the grass-tufted sand dunes that marked the wild western third of San Francisco, when they approached a few wooden buildings—shacks really—in the treeless landscape of 1881.

The tangy salty air breeze came over a dune from the Pacific Ocean as they arrived above Point Lobos. Emma smiled as she heard seals barking on the rocks just offshore. Sea gulls whirled and screeched. Adolph looked excited as he helped Emma down from the buggy. They walked past a small cottage to the bluff. Below, along the ocean beach that stretched more than 3 miles south, hundreds of birds fed furiously, running across the sand just ahead of the tide. On weekends San Francisco's wealthy citizens would race horses on the flat sands, but today, the beach was deserted.

Looking west from their bluff, the Sutros saw a structure perched on a rugged cliff. For visitors who made the journey to eat or watch dance-hall entertainment, the building's "Cliff House" sign seemed to mark the end of civilization.

Then and there, Adolph Sutro decided to buy Sam Tetlow's cottage and build his new house on the bluff above the Cliff House, with gardens to accent and frame the Pacific Ocean views. He told Emma that the Cliff House would be much grander, too. He felt that San Franciscans should have inspiring gardens to walk in and a place to swim—a destination for a wholesome good time, away from the city's industry and day-to-day problems. Sutro remarked, "These western shores should become the lands of cultured groves and artistic gardens, the home of a powerful and refined race. To reach this happy consummation a taste for the beautiful in nature must be engendered among the masses. . . ."

After the buggy ride back to bustling San Francisco, Adolph Sutro immediately bought 1,000 acres of land on the bluff, including the Cliff House and the flatter shoreline land just north. Where others saw worthless rocks, sand, and dunes, he saw opportunity.

In 1850, with his mother and nine brothers and sisters, Sutro had left Aachen, Germany, and the remnants of his dead father's clothing manufacturing business. Twenty years old and restless, Sutro arrived in New York and quickly followed Gold Rush fever to San Francisco. Over the next decade he owned three profitable tobacco shops.

Sutro sold out and took his money to Virginia City, Nevada, in 1860, where Comstock Lode silver mines were creating overnight millionaires. Mining investors and bank owners wanted to use their railroads to haul ore from the mountains. They tried to block "Crazy Sutro" from building a 3.8-mile-long ventilation and drainage tunnel that Sutro claimed would make ore removal safer. Sutro's tunnel did work when it opened in 1878, and the tunnel construction company shares made investors rich. After Sutro lost two elections for Nevada senator in 1880, he sold his tunnel company stock and returned to San Francisco a millionaire.

Fifty years old and a rich man, Sutro was ready to buy property and build a home. Sutro's conviction that people who weren't rich needed to enjoy themselves was unusual; he intended to use his money and land investments to provide for the people.

Lawns and formal flower gardens that changed color with the seasons surrounded Sutro's cottage-style mansion on the Sutro Heights Park bluff. A white glass conservatory protected delicate plants. Two seated stone lions with flowing manes guarded the gates of the property. Classic-style sculptures with winged beasts and goddesses were imported from Belgium. Live monkeys and deer could be glimpsed through the salt-tolerant trees Sutro had imported from Australia.

Sutro's home was filled with more than 100,000 books that he anticipated as the beginning of the world's largest private library—a library for the people of San Francisco. A parapet looked west while Inspiration Point walkway had a view of the Cliff House. The grounds were open to the public for strolling, looking out from the observatory, watching seals on the rocks, or recording the excursion with a photograph. The rich and famous would arrive to stand on Dolce Far Niente (Sweet to Do Nothing) Balcony with Mayor Adolph Sutro. Sutro had finally succeeded in politics, winning on San Francisco's Populist Party ticket in 1894, with promises to break up the Southern Pacific Railroad's transportation monopoly.

To finance his philanthropy and building schemes, Sutro invested in San Francisco land, eventually owning 12 percent of city property. When other railway owners balked at cheap prices for citizens' beach excursions, Sutro, with his hatred of rail monopolies, built his own red-and-white electric trolley line and charged a reasonable 5-cent fare.

The original 1863 Cliff House that provided the masses a place to eat burned in 1894. It was the excuse that Sutro needed to spend $50,000 on an eight-story French Chateau in the seaside-style of San Diego's Hotel del Coronado. Photography and art galleries, a gem collection, windows 200 feet above the water, and the Seal Rocks drew people to its restaurants and souvenir shops.

But the Sutro Baths north of the Cliff House were his pride and joy. In March 1896 a beaming Sutro opened his $600,000 indoor bathhouse, the world's largest. Seven thousand people had taken Sutro's trolley to the beach to try Sutro's "health-giving amusement," as he called it. Sutro wore a white hat that accented his large tufts of white cheek whiskers and looked benevolently at the first swimmers to arrive.

The multi-story glass bathhouse could hold 25,000 people in its bleachers and pools. Using Sutro's own tunnel-like design, high and low tides filled and emptied the 1,685,000 gallons of seawater used to fill and refresh seven pools. A swimmer could choose from a freshwater pool, salt-water pool at ocean temperature, or five other pools heated to temperatures in between.

Entrance was 10 cents, and swimmers paid 25 cents. Detail-oriented Sutro chose the black wool prototype for the swimsuits and towels that the swimmers rented. Time spent on the seven water slides, diving boards, and trapeze cost a few extra cents.

Sutro's Aztec, Mexican, Syrian, Chinese, Japanese, and Egyptian art and craft collections, including mummies and swords, were in display cases. His natural history collection contained preserved animals and mounted insects to entertain children. Performers played to an amphitheatre crowd of 3,700 while restaurants fed the masses.

Swimmers and nonswimmers alike would benefit from Sutro's "amusement and instruction."

By 1898 Sutro was dead. Sutro Heights remained a popular park for decades, but the plaster sculptures deteriorated and the flower gardens died off. Sutro's cottage mansion crumbled into ruins, and his collection of books burned in 1906.

Adolph Sutro's Cliff House was still standing after the 1906 Earthquake, but burned a year later. Emma built a new, simpler Cliff House for her father's beloved public in 1909. Over time, it became run down, was sold, acquired by the National Park Service, and then restored to Emma's Neo-Classic architecture in 2004 as part of the Golden Gate National Recreation Area.

For years Sutro Baths drew thousands of swimmers and pleasure seekers. But without Sutro, the heart of the operation was gone. Some pool area was converted into an ice skating rink in 1937. Eventually the building decayed and land developers began clearing the space in 1964. Two years later a fire transformed the Sutro Baths foundations into today's sea-lapped ruins.

RESCUE IN CHINATOWN

– 1895 –

THE NEW SEWING MISTRESS AT the Presbyterian Occidental Mission Home for Girls in Chinatown was tall, white, unmarried, and observant. It was 1895, and the young sewing teacher, Donaldina MacKenzie Cameron, had decided to walk through Chinatown's back alleys after dark.

Even most San Francisco policemen wouldn't venture down those alleys, fearing that they would not come out of Chinatown alive. No one peering at the woman from a narrow doorway or a balcony among the congestion of multistory wooden houses would be able to tell if she was frightened for her own safety.

The woman was looking around carefully and listening for signs and sounds of women and girls. She was a missionary on a rescue mission. A friend had suggested that the twenty-five-year-old New Zealand–born rancher's daughter spend some time helping Director Maggie Culbertson with the Chinese and other Asian girls who lived at the mission home. Culbertson's mission was to save the girls from prostitution and rehabilitate them.

Donaldina Cameron grew up in central California's rural San Joaquin Valley. She was looking for something to do. The Occidental Mission Home for Girls, a safe house for Chinese girls who had been abused, was in the state's most populous and lively city. Cameron volunteered to help for a while.

She had plunged into learning the culture of San Francisco's Chinatown with its crowded streets and smells of fish, cooked rice, urine, and incense. Cameron saw mostly Chinese men. She also noted porters carrying heavy baskets suspended from a bamboo pole across the shoulders. Those who could afford silk wore it, but cotton jackets and loose trousers were the everyday wear. Men wore long black hair in a queue, a braid that Chinese law forbade them to cut. Shopkeepers watched the world walk by, and merchants yelled as they supervised the unpacking of goods from China and produce from other areas of California.

Some young men loitering in the streets looked menacing. They were probably members of a tong, a kind of hoodlum association formed by people who had the same jobs and were loyal to a single leader. Cameron's recent acquaintance, a new arrival from Germany and children's tutor, Arnold Genthe, loved to photograph Tangrenbu, as he called Chinatown. Genthe warned Cameron that tong members carried hatchets and other weapons and they knew how to use them.

Since the enactment of the Chinese Exclusion Act in 1882, the law excluded the Chinese from entering the United States if they were laborers. Few Chinese wives and women were permitted to legally immigrate to America. Cameron knew that Congress and the courts had decided to keep out Chinese and other "Orientals" who might take work away from European immigrants.

Cameron was not technically a missionary, but she agreed with her church's missionary goal to Christianize those considered heathens, including the Chinese. Maggie Culbertson quickly initiated

Cameron into the mission home's plan of action. Chinese women and girls who were prostitutes or slaves were to be rescued from their squalid quarters, protected, educated, and converted to Christianity. The white women missionaries were to be their saviors.

Suddenly Culbertson fell ill and died. The Presbyterian Church appointed Cameron, the only other white woman familiar with the operation, as the home's director. She was determined to win the Chinese girls' freedom.

Turbulent politics in China and the policies of its Manchu rulers had left many Chinese and their villages in dire poverty. If a Chinese man could immigrate to the United States, he might make enough money to return home and live in style, or at least pay for a fancy burial of his bones next to his ancestors. The hatred and discrimination the Chinese men faced when they reached the United States and San Francisco led them to live in Chinatown. Under U.S. law, very few Chinese women, even those married to Chinese-American citizens, were permitted to join their husbands.

Because there were so few women, Chinatown's residents formed a bachelor society. Social life revolved around men. Sports teams organized by white San Franciscans, their clubs, and churches were off limits to the Chinese. There was little entertainment available to the bachelor society.

Some men elected to visit opium dens, smoking and reclining on mats set up in the back rooms of stores. Gambling meant elaborate games of numbers such as guessing whether button-sized markers were black or white. The gambling den always made a profit. Lotteries were also common. And temples on the upper floors of buildings were a place where gamblers sought to get lucky by burning sticks of incense for joss, to the god, goddess, or Buddha sitting atop the altar.

And there were the girls. Some fathers in China, where girls were believed to be of little value in comparison to boys, sold girl children as young as one year old to slave dealers who in turn imported the girls to the United States. Some girls were forced to sign contracts that promised more time in service for every day they were sick or unable to engage in prostitution, thus insuring they would be enslaved for life. Some girls were sold to the highest bidder on arrival or promised work as household help but in reality were forced to work as prostitutes to stay alive. A few went on to own houses of prostitution themselves.

Typically, two to six girls would live together in a sparsely furnished 12-foot by 6-foot shack divided by heavy curtains into two rooms. A barred window in a small door offered the only entrance and view out. To solicit customers, the girls would call or sing out to passersby. If they couldn't attract and please customers, they might be branded, beaten, or lashed with whips. Many were infected with disease. It was the girls' living quarters and their cries that Cameron had been looking and listening for on her nighttime walk around Chinatown.

Cameron developed a method: Find the girls; get into their small living space, preferably under cover of darkness and with a companion and police backup; persuade them to follow her; and then run back to the home at top speed. Tall, pale, and intimidating, she became legendary for her ability to navigate the narrow dangerous alleys and to escape over the roofs of Chinatown. She received death threats from the tongs that called her Fan Quai, White Devil.

Cameron is credited with saving more than 3,000 Chinatown women and girls from slavery. She escorted the girls to the Mission Home, where they were washed, dressed, and medically examined. Her rescued girls were educated and instructed in Christian doctrine. They called her *Lo Mo,* or Beloved Mother.

The 1906 Earthquake leveled much of Chinatown and destroyed most of Chinatown's prostitution. It also destroyed the Mission

Home building, though Cameron ran back into the advancing fire that had followed the quake to pull her girls' guardianship records from the rubble—the only proof that they were under her care and not slaves.

The Mission Home was rebuilt in 1908. After many years of lobbying, Cameron was overjoyed when the California Legislature abolished "yellow and white prostitution" in 1914. In 1942 the Occidental Mission Home for Girls was renamed Donaldina Cameron House after the woman who started out a sewing teacher but ended up staying forty-seven years to rescue Chinatown's abused.

SHAKING INFERNO

- 1906 -

There was an earthquake hit us at 5.13 this morning,
wrecking several buildings and wrecking our offices.
They are carting dead from the fallen buildings. Fire
all over town. There is no water and we lost our power.
I'm going to get out of the office, as we have had a little
shake every few minutes, and it's me for the simple life.

—R., SAN FRANCISCO, 5.50 A.M.

THE LONE POSTAL TELEGRAPH COMPANY SIGNALMAN who used his initial, R, was on duty in downtown San Francisco early on April 18, 1906. It was then that a mighty earthquake trembled, sixty seconds of terrifying shaking. Afterwards no one could agree if the quaking started at 5:11, 5:12, or 5:13 A.M., but after a while it no longer mattered. In the end, destructive fires burned what the earthquake had not destroyed.

The immediate goal for San Franciscans was survival. Those thrown from their beds or making early morning milk, produce, or newspaper deliveries by wagon were soon to join the throngs of the richest and poorest people running through the streets, fleeing crumbling masonry, cracks in the street, and the fires that destroyed more than half of San Francisco's buildings.

To locals and visitors like Italian opera star, Enrico Caruso, who was tossed out of bed in his Palace Hotel suite by nature's jolts, it seemed like the world had come down around them. Chinatown crumbled like a pack of cards, said one observer. The Chinese who weren't buried under rubble banged gongs and noisemakers to fend off bad spirits.

San Francisco Examiner editor P. Barrett and two colleagues left work as the 5 A.M. sun was beginning to burn through the fog on Market Street. A joke between the three hung in the air as the earth slipped away and the men staggered before being thrown on their faces. Barrett saw the newspaper buildings and skyscrapers dancing around him, sending up wooden timbers and gray dust. He heard a roaring sound as structures crumbled, jangling glass shattered, and raining masonry thudded into the ruined streets. Streetcar tracks were warped and twisted and the raw ends of electric wires were flung everywhere. Barrett later recalled in horror that "men were on all fours, in the street, like crawling bugs."

San Francisco was no stranger to earthquakes. Mild ones cracked plaster almost daily. Most were imperceptible. Occasionally major quakes toppled buildings and started local fires, but until 1906, none had been so destructive. Most long-term residents were philosophical, expecting that their residence on a rock-based hill would protect them, or that there would be time to grab belongings before a quake caused major damage.

No one expected that an earthquake would be so destructive. It was later estimated to rate 6.9–8.2 on the seismic scale invented in 1935 by Charles Richter. All the frightened inhabitants knew when it struck was that this one was a major temblor.

San Francisco-born writer, Jack London, was living 40 miles north in Santa Rosa when the earthquake struck. He and his wife raced to the city, and *Collier's Weekly,* a major New York magazine, commissioned him to report what he saw:

> *Within an hour after the earthquake shock the smoke*
> *of San Francisco's burning was a lurid tower visible a*
> *hundred miles away. For three days and nights this*
> *lurid tower swayed in the sky, reddening the sun, dark-*
> *ening the day, and filling the land with smoke.*

For four days London wandered downtown and around Nob Hill mansions before and after they burned; he graphically described the firestorm as he observed it and heard of it from people in the street. By late afternoon, twelve hours after the quake struck, London could see that half of the city was gone. While the bay was calm and no wind was blowing, the fire was sucking in air with a whoosh from every direction, creating a "colossal chimney through the atmosphere."

Fires had started immediately, especially south of Market Street where flophouses, taverns, brothels, factories, and warehouses were built of wood. In 1906 fireplaces and stoves consumed wood or coal. Many people without electric wiring still used candles and lanterns. Collapsing buildings caused sparks. Fire was the great enemy, and small fires started quickly in the poor districts.

Nob Hill and Russian Hill residents watched the flames from afar from front gardens where their silver service and china had been brought out for breakfast. A housewife not far from today's Civic Center lit her stove to make breakfast and started what was soon called the Ham and Eggs Fire. The South of Market blazes and Ham and Eggs Fire met and burned through the other neighborhoods and up the posh residential hillsides toward mansions and art collections of Old Masters.

No one had expected that the water mains were corroded and the reservoirs were broken. Firemen and their pumping engines were powerless without water. Brigades of people passing a chain of water-filled buckets were rare. Police and the soldiers summoned from The Presidio rationed what little drinking water there was. The only water source that worked was singer Lotta Crabtree's gift to San Francisco, a fountain at Market and Kearny Streets.

Newly homeless people threw whatever they could into trunks and pulled them through the streets and up hills. Canaries, parrots, cats, and dogs were carried in arms, along with babies who weren't being pushed in strollers. The crowds fled, zigzagging in front of the fires toward green areas like Golden Gate Park and The Presidio. They set up rough camps with tents labeled with occupants' names and former addresses. Many, like Caruso, took the first ferry they could board to Oakland if they had the dime fare.

San Franciscans saw that political corruption had allowed public-works projects to be done shabbily, if at all—the City Hall building, with its elegant dome but unreinforced foundations, was left a shell. The political machine had siphoned money from lucrative contracts to maintain water pipes and sewers. Now San Franciscans' laissez-faire attitudes were returning to haunt them.

The acting Presidio commander, Brigadier General Frederick Funston, ordered U.S. Army soldiers stationed at The Presidio to assist citizens and fight fires. But without water the Army was reduced to trying to set up firebreaks with dynamite.

Funston's troops dynamited street after street until their dynamite supply ran low; they made their last stand at Van Ness Avenue's wide boulevard. Finally, after three days of rubble, fires, and ash rain that produced a weird twilight, the fire line was turned back by dynamite at the east side of Van Ness.

More than 20,000 buildings had been destroyed. In 2005 San Francisco's Board of Supervisors revised the long-standing number of dead from 478 to an unknown number exceeding 3,500.

San Francisco began rebuilding within a few weeks, as dollars flooded in from around the world. This time, more structures were reinforced properly and the water system was strengthened with permanent reservoirs. Every April 18, at 5:12 A.M., 1906 Earthquake and Fire survivors and their descendants gather at Lotta's Fountain to remember.

ELLIS ISLAND OF THE WEST

- 1910 -

Leaving our homeland and floating across the ocean,
we settled in this wooden shed.
Starting from scratch, as Chinese pioneers,
we tried to become established in the Golden Gate

—TRANSLATED FROM CHINESE,
CARVED STONE MONUMENT ON ANGEL ISLAND

THE WOODEN BARRACKS ON AN ISLAND IN San Francisco Bay named for an angel were the same as a prison. Barbed wire surrounded the barracks' sleeping halls and the few other buildings of the Immigration Station that was set up in 1910. Angel Island was a processing center for those who, like European immigrants arriving through Ellis Island in New York, wanted to settle in America.

Unlike most immigrants at Ellis Island, the hopeful masses arriving in San Francisco were primarily from Asia, and the majority was

Chinese. For decades the Chinese had called California *Gam San,* or Gold Mountain. It was a promised land to them, a place where a hard worker could prosper. After accumulating wealth, they would return home to their village in China and upon death would be ceremonially buried with their ancestors.

During California's Gold Rush, Chinese worked the leavings of the goldfields and became small shop owners and laundrymen. In later years the Chinese were the poorly paid labor force that built the Central Pacific Railroad track for Charles Crocker and the Big Four. Many eventually settled in San Francisco's Chinatown.

Much of the hatred and discrimination toward the Chinese began with the Chinese Police Tax enacted by California in 1862, also known as the Anti-Coolie Tax. Dennis Kearney led his Workingman's Association of longshoremen in demonstrations and riots against the use of Chinese laborers along the waterfront in the late 1870s.

In 1882 the U.S. Congress enacted the Chinese Exclusion Act, which prevented any Chinese laborer or miner from legally entering the country and excluded any Chinese from attaining citizenship. Once the Exclusion Act was in force, the Chinese had to present a certificate in English—complete with name, title, official rank, age, height, physical characteristics, former and present occupation, and place of residence in China—to prove that he had never been a laborer or miner.

Anti-Chinese sentiment in San Francisco was heightened when a ship arriving from Hong Kong in 1899 carried two cases of bubonic plague on board. The ship was sent to the quarantine station at Angel Island in 1892. It was easy to land and isolate passengers at the island's Ayala Cove harbor. In 1900 city officials used the plague epidemic as an excuse to quarantine Chinatown. In 1901 they cleaned 1,200 homes and 14,000 Chinatown rooms by force, blaming the Chinese for the plague.

How were the Chinese now going to enter the land of Gold Mountain? One exception to the Exclusion Act restrictions was to prove that an immigrant was a child of American citizens.

After the 1906 Earthquake and Fire ruined San Francisco's records, many Chinese claimed to be citizens. Often, the "proof" was forged papers, and those carrying the documents were derisively called "paper sons" or "paper daughters."

The immigration bureau detained any working-class Chinese upon arrival for detailed questioning, including details about the home village in China and family genealogy. In 1910 the Immigration Station became part of the island already containing a cattle ranch, stone quarry, Civil War army encampment, Indian War recruiting and training site, and quarantine station.

Over the next thirty years, about 175,000 Chinese immigrants were sent to Angel Island. They arrived by ferryboat at the shore of China Cove near the cold Chinese Detention Barracks. They awaited document screening and long interrogations. Two manned towers had guns trained on the barracks at all times, and the compound was surrounded by barbed wire. San Francisco was an hour-long ferry ride away and the distance made escape impossible.

Individuals would stay at the Angel Island Immigration Station from two weeks to nearly two years, depending on their circumstances, before admission into the United States or deportation back to China.

Most Chinese arriving at Angel Island were men, but men and women and even families were separated to keep them from supporting each other's stories during questioning. They slept on bunks that rose up the walls. The women's dormitory had ninety beds; the men's had almost three times as many. There were separate exercise yards. Water was not plentiful and the food was terrible enough to incite food riots in 1919. Boys lured tiny birds with their rice ration and figured out a way to clean and cook them.

The lonely and frightened detainees, terrified of giving a wrong answer or not responding with information that matched their documents, hoped that someone—perhaps a relative already in Chinatown—would give inspectors $1,000 under the table to get relatives processed and off Angel Island. A few men committed suicide. Hundreds of confined men wrote or carved their sorrowful thoughts and poems on the barracks walls. There was little privacy, but the writing in Classic Tang Dynasty Chinese was a source of pride. The poetry, all anonymous, was sad.

My existing circumstances justify my anger.
Sitting here, uselessly delayed for long years and months,
I am like a cuckoo in a cage.

The Chinese were not the only group detained on Angel Island. Japanese nationals and almost 20,000 Japanese picture brides engaged to American men who had seen only their photographs also passed through the Immigration Station. Criminals were locked up in a separate prison on the barracks' second floor before Alcatraz Penitentiary was built. World War I enemy nationals were incarcerated, and even a few Europeans were processed, though very swiftly in comparison.

In 1940 the station's administration building burned down. For the Chinese the 1940s were a different era. World War II would envelop Europe and Asia. China became a United States ally. By 1943 the Chinese Exclusion Act was an embarrassment and was repealed.

CHRISTMAS EVE DIVA

- 1910 -

THE NEW YORK PAPERS WERE FULL OF THE SCANDAL in late 1910: Luisa Tetrazzini was gone! The Manhattan Opera singer from Florence who sang like a nightingale was flagrantly ignoring the filing of a legal injunction, her probable contract, and, in all likelihood, common sense.

The Florentine Nightingale—a play on the name of the famous British nurse, Florence Nightingale—was believed to be en route to San Francisco, the city rebuilt after the 1906 Earthquake and Fire. Tetrazzini had mentioned that she would return to the city where she had received accolades during her 1904 American singing debut. "Cheering crowds lined Market Street all the way from the Ferry Building to the Palace Hotel," one report had raved at the time.

Over the past several years since the 1906 catastrophe, the nation had contributed more than $100 million to resurrect San Francisco's buildings, businesses, and schools. Local residents hoped that the Italian opera singer would show her support, keep her promise, and return to sing to plucky San Franciscans who had been her earliest American fans. Tetrazzini promised big, in the tradition of the saying, "It ain't over till the fat lady sings." Her fun-loving and indulgent personality and appetite established her persona as a buxom diva who was "plump as a spring robin," as one reviewer delicately wrote. Her favorite dish, often shared with equal gusto by her friend and co-star, Enrico Caruso—who had been tossed out of his Palace Hotel bed in San Francisco by the 1906 quake—was spaghetti Tetrazzini. Heavy with pasta, butter, and cream, the chicken and turkey Tetrazzini dishes named for her delighted the prima donna. Indulgence sometimes forced her to leave off her corset for performances to the shock of the audience and the giggles of male opera stars trying to support her during duets. Luisa handled it all with good humor, telling a German soprano, "Some singers gotta da figure, but Tetrazzini gotta da voice!"

A very high soprano she had. In her era Tetrazzini was the most famous coloratura soprano with the ability to hit high notes even after an elephant-sized meal. Born in Florence in 1871, she debuted there at age nineteen. She became famous outside Italy during a decade in South America and Russia, though she craved the fame a debut at London Covent Garden would bring. Before she startled London critics with her operatic skill and impossibly high range in 1907, she had tested the waters in the United States, singing with the San Francisco Opera. A mutual admiration formed between city and singer.

In the decades that followed the Gold Rush, many singers had a following in the waterfront dance halls and saloons of what came to be called the Barbary Coast. San Franciscans had loved culture, dancers, songstresses, and opera singers. Lola Montez, infamous as the one-time mistress of both composer Franz Liszt and King Ludwig I of Bavaria, had first performed her racy "Spider Dance" in San Francisco in May 1853. That same year, Lola began teaching a young redheaded neighbor in Grass Valley (Northern California Gold Country) to sing and dance. By 1856, Lola's petite nine-year-old protégé, Lotta Crabtree, had moved from the mining camps to the dance palaces and concert halls of San Francisco, where Mother Crabtree gathered up the gold nuggets thrown onstage. Miss Lotta, "San Francisco's Favorite," as she was fondly known, was rich when still a teenager from land she bought up all over downtown.

Lotta, like Tetrazzini, never forgot her first fans. On September 9, 1875, a tall, bronze-colored drinking fountain donated by Lotta Crabtree was dedicated on Market Street. The intersection where Kearny, Geary, and 3rd Streets met was a gathering place for shoppers, workers, and commuters. The two-story-high cast-iron Beaux-Arts fountain with a column rising from its base was a convenient landmark, a meeting place that anyone could find. San Francisco's major newspapers eventually built offices on the three intersecting corners.

On April 18, 1906, Lotta's Fountain was one of the few downtown spots that remained undamaged after the Great Earthquake. It provided water to fight the Great Fire. Within hours of the quake, Lotta Crabtree's gift to the city was the place for San Franciscans to meet and to discover who was missing, injured, or dead, who had fled the city, or who was camping out in one of the city parks.

Four years later it seemed that San Francisco's favorite coloratura soprano was going to come back to San Francisco. After the 1907 Covent Garden success, New York wanted her. When the Metropolitan Opera, an institution in New York, hesitated, she was recruited by the rival Manhattan Opera's Oscar Hammerstein. All seemed well until Hammerstein was hired away by the Metropolitan Opera. Where Luisa was under contract was disputed by both opera companies. In 1910 Hammerstein held her to the contract and sued to obtain an injunction that required the diva to remain in New York and prevented her from singing anywhere else for that season.

Suddenly the opera singer was nowhere to be found. Though an injunction was never issued by a court, Tetrazzini defiantly told the New York press, "I will sing in San Francisco if I have to sing there in the streets, for I know the streets of San Francisco are free!"

Christmas was approaching and the air was chilly in San Francisco. When holiday shoppers patronizing the stores on Kearny Street stepped onto Market Street to catch a streetcar, they saw a commotion around Lotta's Fountain. It appeared that workmen were constructing a platform close to the fountain that was topped by a bright streetlamp. Could it be for her?

By Christmas Eve, the word was out. The Florentine Nightingale was in San Francisco and would sing at Lotta's Fountain. In an age before microphones and amplifiers, her voice would have to carry for several blocks.

As the light faded, the diva, dressed in white with a huge white hat on her head, faced Lotta's Fountain and began to sing. She trilled through popular songs and a waltz from the opera, *Romeo and Juliet.* The high, clear tones of Luisa Tetrazzini's cheerful, melodious voice (so papers reported the next morning) had enthralled 250,000 people standing in the streets of San Francisco.

PANAMA CONNECTION

- 1915 -

THOMAS DOYLE, SAN FRANCISCO'S OFFICIAL Noise Committee chairman, had waited for February 20, 1915, to arrive for a long time. The city would strut its stuff when the Panama-Pacific International Exposition opened that day. It was almost 6:00 A.M. and the sky was still dark. Eager marchers would be assembling at Van Ness Avenue and Broadway.

The city was about to hear Doyle's wake-up call, the signal to the rest of the country that San Francisco had fully recovered from the 1906 Earthquake and Fire. At precisely 6:00 A.M., firehouses sounded their alarms, trolleys clanged bells, and businesses set off whistles and horns. The Fife and Drum Corps made as much noise as possible. Frank Morton Todd later remembered "an appalling din which had something primordial and soul-shaking in it."

San Franciscans had had enough shaking with the 1906 Earthquake, but planning for San Francisco's second exposition had actually begun earlier, in 1904, when the Panama Canal building project had gotten under way. Years before, the French had unsuccessfully tried to build a canal. President Teddy Roosevelt was determined that America was to build and finish it.

Many Gold Rush prospectors and others San Francisco-bound had to go "around the Horn" at the southern tip of South America or endure malaria and a harrowing trek across the Isthmus of Panama at the narrowest point in Central America. If a Panama Canal could be built, a ship traveling from New York to San Francisco could shave 7,872 miles off the ocean journey.

San Francisco decided to lobby the U.S. government to be the site of an exposition on the latest in technology, industry, and exotic foreign displays; it would also tie in with the opening of the last link to the West—the Panama Canal. Other rivals bid as early as 1904: Baltimore, Washington, D.C., Boston, and New Orleans. The latter pitched itself as the first port stop on the way to the canal. San Diego also lobbied to be the first port after canal transit opened; the city commenced building Balboa Park as its proposed venue.

San Francisco's quick earthquake recovery and promise not to demand federal funds won the city the exposition in 1911. People remembered the 1894 Midwinter Exposition in Golden Gate Park where exhibits coming by train had been delayed by weather in the Rocky Mountains, so local planners vowed that the city's second exposition would open on time—and all would be ready.

Rubble from the 1906 earthquake was hauled to the waterfront east of San Francisco's Presidio, and the marshland was filled in. The exposition's 635 acres—seventy-six city blocks between Van Ness Avenue, the Presidio, and the newly filled shoreline of San Francisco Bay and Chestnut Street—would be filled with fountains, exhibition halls designed by famous architects, and an entertainment zone. Thousands of works of art would also be on display.

Marshall Hale, who was in charge of the opening-day parade, observed the excited, noisy crowd assembling in packed, orderly rows at Van Ness Avenue. He had spent months telling civic groups:

We are going out there on the morning of February 20 to open OUR Exposition. We want everybody. We shall walk. No carriages, no automobiles, everybody on foot without distinction, led by our Mayor, just the people of San Francisco.

The 6:00 A.M. racket started and Mayor "Sunny Jim" Rolph began walking quickly. He was almost running. Hale sprinted toward Rolph to tell him to slow down enough for the six carriages of early city pioneers and an estimated 150,000 ordinary San Franciscans to catch up.

When they arrived at the exposition, they saw in eight carefully chosen pastel colors a wonderland of towers, orangish domes, and splashing fountains. At the Scott Street main entrance was the centerpiece, the 435-foot-high Tower of Jewels. Higher by far than the other buildings, the tower was hung with 102,000 pieces of free-hanging cut glass backed by mirrors for enhanced shimmer. In the early morning light, the aquamarine, ruby, emerald, sapphire, yellow, and clear gems fluttered and glowed. At night a hidden bank of fifty-four spotlights made the Novagems, as they were called, glow without distracting shadows.

Eleven exhibit halls called palaces showcased everything from agriculture to mining, manufacturing to bread making, as well as the latest inventions by the Singer Sewing Machine Company. Underwood's working model typewriter at the Palace of Liberal Arts weighed 14 tons. Publisher William Randolph Hearst had contributed a giant color press to exhibit printing of the *San Francisco Examiner.*

Architect Bernard R. Maybeck designed the Palace of Fine Arts as a Roman-style colonnade with a rotunda and regal white swans swimming by its lagoon reflection. His fine arts palace would hold 11,400 paintings and sculptures by living artists.

Each of the forty-eight states had a pavilion. Virginia reproduced Mount Vernon; Ohio replicated its state house without a dome; Oregon used redwood tree trunks for its Parthenon pillars; and Philadelphia sent the Liberty Bell. Foreign nations also had palaces.

Exotic South Seas Samoa astounded *Little House on the Prairie* author Laura Ingalls Wilder, when she visited the exposition's Fun Zone amusement park on the east side. Joseph B. Strauss, who would later be the Golden Gate Bridge chief engineer, built the Fun Zone Aeroscope, a cantilever-manipulated structure resembling the Eiffel Tower in Paris. Passengers, 118 at once, boarded the observation car at ground level and were swung 330 feet above the exposition for a fine view of tower tops and the bay. In addition, a five-acre exhibit simulated transit through the Panama Canal.

Biplane pilots performed acrobatics over the water. On the west side of the Presidio track, Wilder was enchanted with the Kentucky race and horse riding. A steady stream of celebrities, politicians, and movie stars were on the scene to be seen and photographed.

The Panama-Pacific International Exposition fantasy world of towers and domes closed on December 4. After it concluded, planners intended the plaster and burlap-style material used for temporary building exteriors to crumble and disintegrate in the wind and fog. Almost all of the buildings disappeared or were taken down to clear space for later development.

San Francisco did keep a few souvenirs, and among them, Bernard Maybeck's Palace of Fine Arts. The innovative Exploratorium science museum took up residence in a section of the Palace of Fine Arts in 1969 after the entire building was permanently rebuilt in cement. It survived not only the elements, but also the 1989 Loma Prieta Earthquake. The destruction that ravaged the Marina District buildings in 1989 was caused by unstable landfill from the 1915 exposition—rubble from the 1906 earthquake.

DEATH OF A PRESIDENT

- 1923 -

THE STAFF AT THE PALACE HOTEL WAS IN A flurry of preparation. The hotel management had heard that the twenty-ninth U.S. President, Warren G. Harding, wanted rest upon arrival in San Francisco. Busily they went about preparing his room and arranging flowers.

As soon as Harding arrived at the train station, he was quickly seated in a limousine for the ride to San Francisco's prestigious Market Street hotel. The president and his wife, Florence Kling de Wolfe Harding, whom the president wryly called "Duchess," for her strong and commanding personality, were both recovering from summer illnesses. The fifty-seven-year-old Harding had been sick with bouts of the flu, but he had insisted that they take the train from Washington, D.C., to the West Coast and then from there onto a long-anticipated cruise to Alaska. He would finish the trip with an official duty—a speech in San Francisco about the World Court. The presidential entourage departed the capital in June 1923. When he was up to it, Harding gave speeches and shook hands everywhere they stopped along the way on what was dubbed the "Voyage of Understanding."

When Harding was too tired, Duchess gave his speeches from the train platform, and no one seemed to mind. The United States had emerged from World War I victorious and determined to enjoy its post-war prosperity. Harding's amiable personality made him popular. Pushed by the ambitious Duchess, the former Marion, Ohio, newspaper publisher and Ohio senator had won the presidency on the Republican ticket and was sworn in on March 4, 1921.

President Harding's host in San Francisco was to be "Sunny Jim" Rolph, the post-earthquake mayor who was in the middle of what would be nineteen years as the city's leader. Like Harding, James Rolph Jr. was smiling and relaxed in public and genuinely liked making contact with people. People seldom remembered exactly what the mayor said or meant, just that he smiled and exuded confidence similar to Harding's self-described "bloviation"—speaking lots of words without deep meaning. It helped that the ever-cheerful mayor dressed nattily, wore a flower in his lapel, and loved his shiny cowboy boots.

The Harding party was arriving in a city where doors were seldom locked and citizens, well recovered from the earthquake and fires of 1906, enjoyed a good party. Rolph made sure the new City Hall and other white Civic Center buildings shone.

After the 18th Amendment was added to the constitution early in 1920, Prohibition was in effect, but that didn't stop illegal moonshiners, winemakers, and speakeasies from making a profit on alcohol. Republican "Sunny Jim" made sure delegates at the Democratic Convention at the city's new Civic Auditorium in 1920 were well supplied with bottles of bourbon handed to them by local women.

In 1920 ratification of the 19th Amendment enfranchised women to vote. By 1923 the Roaring 20s had revved up. Dresses had shortened and women were bobbing their hair and smoking in public alongside men. Everyone was listening to jazz music that had arrived on the West Coast along with frenetic dances like the Charleston.

President Harding, who liked to drink, chew tobacco, and play poker privately with friends, was sick on arrival in San Francisco. Two White House doctors diagnosed him with ptomaine poisoning from bad clams on the Alaska cruise. The doctors ordered that Harding be on bed rest, in case his heart was enlarged. The entourage skipped a Portland stop to arrive in San Francisco. Dr. Ray Lyman Wilbur, president of both Stanford University and the American Medical Association, was there to greet them with a renowned cardiologist.

What the outsiders didn't know was that President Harding's government appointments were beginning to backfire. Harding, who was proud of opening the windows and curtains of the White House so that the people could see in, had failed to cover up details of what would become full-blown scandals after he died. His Veterans Bureau director sold veterans hospital supplies and was caught siphoning off hospital construction fees, and the Veterans Bureau auditor committed suicide. Harding had been content to ignore the deals to sell oil from the national oil reserves to the major United States oil companies, a scandal that would be called Teapot Dome after the Wyoming land formation that held a major oil reserve. Moreover, Harding's campaign manager had been appointed attorney general, and administration critics were harassed by a corrupt FBI director. Finally, Harding's many mistresses were paid their blackmail money demands to keep his secrets.

Meanwhile, a sick and worried president was in bed in San Francisco. His aides had cancelled public engagements. Eventually, Harding was able to read the papers, chat, and be propped up in bed. Reporters hovered outside the presidential suite. His four doctors advised rest until he was well enough to travel directly back to Washington.

Harding was in bed at 7:00 P.M. on August 2, 1923. The Duchess was reading to him. She may have left the room as his nurse came in to give him medication. No one could agree who was in the room when Harding took his last breath. The doctors or a doctor may have been present—or maybe not. The big question was where did Mrs. Harding, the Duchess, go?

By 7:35 P.M. when one of the White House doctors arrived, Harding's white-robed dead body was flat on the bed, prepared by some unknown person. Was the Duchess involved with her husband's death? Did she want to hide the graft he was worried about, or was she simply tired of the other women in his life? Regardless, the doctors pronounced that the president had died from a stroke.

Harding did return directly to Washington, D.C., by train after all, his casket seen by thousands of mourners lining the tracks. The Duchess would not permit an autopsy and burned Warren G. Harding's papers with the body immediately after she returned by train to Washington, D.C. Meanwhile, Mayor Rolph's San Francisco mourned the president's death and then returned to enjoying the Roaring Twenties.

BLOODY THURSDAY

- 1934 -

"WHARF RAT" LONGSHOREMEN HOWARD SPERRY and Nicolas Bordoise lay in their pooling blood at Mission and Steuart Streets. The two were clearly dead, shot by tense San Francisco policemen armed with revolvers and riot guns. More bullets had simultaneously bloodied thirty-one other longshoremen. Enraged male dockworkers, stevedores, sailors, and longshoremen, armed with stones and bricks, surged toward the uniformed police who had pushed them north of the piers along The Embarcadero near the Ferry Building.

The day before, the whole city had taken a breath and celebrated Independence Day 1934. It was during the Great Depression and a holiday—even an unpaid one—was welcome. The remaining days of July that year were anything but peaceful.

Since May 9, Sperry and Bordoise, along with 16,000 other West Coast waterfront workers, had been on strike against shipowners. The strike, originally called for March 23, was postponed while President Franklin D. Roosevelt's fact-finding board tried to find a resolution between workers and shipowners. No solution was found, and at dawn on May 9, longshoremen gathered but did not report for work at the piers and waterfront sheds.

In the early 1930s a longshoreman desperate for work paid bribes to get a job that paid $.75 per hour for an 8 A.M. to midnight shift. Longshoremen were starving and living in dark, one-room, unheated flats. Waterfront work was notoriously unsafe without laws to protect the workers unloading and loading the ships that docked and sailed from major ports. It cost an employer less if a longshoreman died on the job than if an accident maimed someone, who then had to be supported for life.

Bosses were demanding, and existing unions were weak and controlled by the shipping companies. A longshoreman was hired for each day or by the job and had to stand in line to receive a work assignment. He paid a company hiring agent to get the job, then worked long hours until his feet and hands bled. The system included men who were better paid and belonged in "Star Gangs": 1,000 or so elite workers on the San Francisco waterfront who toiled faster and earned more than the 3,000 other "casual" workers. Whenever a strike ensued, shipowners easily found other workers—strikebreakers—to fill in. Back in 1919 the steamship owners had crushed a local attempt to organize a San Francisco maritime workers' union.

Early in 1934, bribes, kickbacks, brutal working conditions, long hours, and lack of overtime pay infuriated Australia-born labor activist Harry Bridges. The resurgence of the International Longshoreman's Association (ILA), a union that was controlled by the shipowners, was the latest affront. Bridges was ready to face off with the dominant Waterfront Employers' Association. Maritime workers demanded a six-hour workday, a thirty-hour week, a $1 hourly wage, an independent union-run hiring hall, and a West Coast longshoremen contract.

Harry Bridges was an experienced nineteen-year-old civilian sailor when he arrived in San Francisco on a schooner in 1920. Bridges wanted to settle down ashore and soon became a longshoreman in the Star Gang. Bridges had to pay dues to the Longshoreman's Association of San Francisco and the Bay Region, the union everyone called the Blue Book Union. To keep his job, Bridges had to compete with the other men and load more and more cargo per hour. In 1934 the shipowners knew that workers were desperate for waterfront jobs and expected to easily deny union demands and break any strike as easily as they had in 1919.

Bridges, known for his liberalism, honesty, wit, and suspected Communist Party membership, spent every free minute walking the waterfront and drinking with workingmen in the bars. He said he was a "working stiff," just like they were, and talked about wages and unions and democracy. Bridges's strong statements about waterfront workers' rights made him a potential target for blacklisting or outright firing by the shipowners.

The Depression had meant less profit for shipowners who by 1934 depended on federal government subsidies to pay their expenses. Spoiling food left on the docks and goods not moving to market during the strike were chalking up a daily $700,000 loss for San Francisco's shipowners and creating an economic nightmare for one of the United States' major ports.

Shipowners demanded that the Port of San Francisco be reopened. Mayor Angelo J. Rossi ordered the city police force to help defend strikebreakers who were hired by the Atlas Trucking Company; they rolled their trucks through Pier 38's doors on July 3. A riot broke out with "fist fights and popping of tear gas guns and bombs," reported the *San Francisco News*. It took eighteen round trips to move bird seed, cocoa beans, and tires from Pier 38 to a warehouse.

After the July 4 respite, crowds gathered and police prepared for another riot on July 5. Royce Brier of the *San Francisco Chronicle* reported that when the thirty-three longshoremen were shot "blood ran red in the streets of San Francisco." On July 6, the *San Francisco Call-Bulletin* reported that "Red Roses—and blood, mementoes of San Francisco's 'bloody Thursday' . . ." lay where Sperry and Bordoise had died.

After thousands joined the nearly silent funeral cortège escorted by a union band and shuffling feet, San Franciscans who had not taken sides swung to the side of the waterfront workers. The Teamsters Union and sixty-three other unions voted in support of a general strike.

A three-day general strike began at 8 A.M. on Monday July 16 in part to protest the state militia guarding the waterfront. Grocery stores, restaurants, and gas stations closed. San Francisco's business activity ground to a halt. Mayor Rossi feared lawlessness and Communist activity and requested that California Governor Frank Merriam send additional national guardsmen to defend the waterfront.

Harry Bridges and the waterfront workers sensed that they had won and each day allowed more San Francisco business and daily activity to return to normal. On October 12 arbitration awarded the union a wage of $.95 per hour, a six-hour workday, thirty-hour week, overtime pay, a coastwide labor contract, and a hiring hall operated by the union.

The general strike was over. Working stiff Harry Bridges went on to found the International Longshoremen's and Warehousemen's Union (ILWU) in San Francisco 1937 and was its president for 40 years—all because two wharf rats died on Bloody Thursday.

CHINA CLIPPER

- 1935 -

On a clear afternoon in late November 1935, Pan American Airways's newest flying boat, the *China Clipper,* sat with its riveted aluminum belly in San Francisco Bay. Firmly anchored in the former yacht basin at Pan Am's West Coast base in Alameda, the 53,000-pound Martin M-130 airplane, with its 130-foot wingspan, was Pan Am President Juan Terry Trippe's latest shrewd gamble.

West of Trippe and the 25,000 spectators standing dockside, was the aircraft he believed could span the Pacific Ocean for the first time. Westward stretched the towers of the unfinished San Francisco–Oakland Bay Bridge. Beyond were San Francisco's piers, Coit Tower perched on Telegraph Hill, and 150,000 San Franciscans hoping to witness history.

This November 22, all eyes were on Trippe. The Yale-educated diplomat was a persuasive, sometimes ruthless visionary, legendary for getting what he wanted. He hired the best engineers and pilots, including Charles Lindbergh as a consultant. He lobbied and cajoled

Washington insiders. Trippe initiated bidding and engineering battles between major airplane manufacturers like Sikorsky, Martin,
and Boeing.

In the 1920s Trippe had cornered the contracts with the United
States Post Office to carry letters by air to Cuba, the Caribbean, and
South America. Airmail was a very big business. A letter sent in airmail cargo took days rather than weeks to reach its destination. A
stamp for a one-ounce letter cost $.03, and a post card stamp cost
$.01. Airmail in the United States cost $.06. Overseas airmail postage
could cost four times as much, and Trippe was determined to expand
Pan Am's airmail profits on new routes.

As head of the world's largest international aviation company
that carried airmail, cargo, and passengers, Trippe's monopoly in the
western hemisphere had recently been denied access to European and
British airfields. French, British, and other airlines were behind in
developing long-range aircraft and did not want challenges from
America. Trippe's decision was bold: go much farther than on the
East Coast–to–Europe route by starting a transpacific route to
China. The aircraft designers wondered how they would accomplish
this feat. The fastest flying boats could fly no more than 3,200 miles
without servicing and refueling.

Trippe's own research led him to study the swift nineteenth-
century clipper ships that had made trade with the Far East and
China very profitable before steamships, especially for cargo that
needed to be delivered quickly. He dubbed his new flying boats
clippers. Once airmail was delivered, luxury passenger service could
be introduced.

To the shock of his staff, Trippe decided they would fly the four-
engine, nonpressurized flying boat 8,200 miles from San Francisco
Bay to Manila in the Philippines with one ton of airmail. In March
1935 a Pan Am cargo ship had sailed through the Golden Gate to

Hawaii, Midway, Wake, and Guam with materiel and supplies to build airstrips and facilities for the jumps west over the Pacific.

Now, standing calmly, watching veteran pilot Ed Musick and his crew board the 90-foot-long *China Clipper,* Trippe told him, "Captain Musick, you have your sailing orders. Cast off and depart for Manila in accordance therewith."

Musick and his crew would not dare to sleep much for fear of going off course as they navigated the first 2,400 miles to Honolulu. The 111,000 airmail letters carried on the inaugural flight were stamped at $.25 for each segment, or $.75 per one-half ounce for a letter addressed from San Francisco to Manila. Pan Am earned a decent return, and the publicity would be priceless—if they succeeded.

The *China Clipper's* engines started up accompanied by the singing of *The Star Spangled Banner.* The roar of the crowd in Alameda drifted west across the bay and was matched with sirens, car horns, and noisemakers in San Francisco.

The metal belly slowly began to clear the water, only to be faced with dangling cables from the Bay Bridge construction. The crowd watched and figured it was a typical air-show stunt when Musick slowly aimed the nose *through* the cables and hanging metal before pulling clear of the debris. Soon the *China Clipper* was on its way over the other bridge being constructed over the bay, the Golden Gate Bridge.

Flying speed ranged from 125 to 160 miles per hour. At Pearl Harbor in Honolulu, a cheering crowd of 3,000 people waited on November 23. At Midway chief engineer C. D. Wright radioed, "We got up with the gooney birds this morning at a quarter to four. . . . The lagoon was calm in the tropic dawn as Captain Musick gave our 3,200 horses [horsepower from four engines] their heads, and the goonies flapped up with shrill screams at their roar."

From Wake Island, Wright assured the bosses at the Alameda base, "Our veteran skippers and crew men, and the complete facilities of our bases strung across this big ocean make a flight like this seem as safe as a train to a suburb—as it is."

By November 26 Pan American Airways Radio was reporting that the International Date Line had been crossed. Wright noted, "Almost before we notice it is tomorrow. We don't feel any older, but our instruments show us we have flashed over the international date line, out of Monday into Tuesday. It's a funny idea. What is this time anyway? The same sun is shining that glinted off our wings as we lifted from the lagoon at Midway, but it's Tuesday's sun now when it was Monday's then."

On November 29 the *China Clipper* landed in Manila. Musick and his crew had inaugurated transpacific airmail service by flying 8,210 miles in fifty-nine hours and forty-eight minutes. Almost as many letters returned to San Francisco when the *China Clipper* soared over the bay to Alameda on December 6, 1935. Onward flights to Hong Kong, an entrée to China, soon followed.

Trippe's M-130 *Hawaii Clipper* repeated the feat on October 21, 1936. San Francisco to Manila passengers paid $799 one way for the privilege of flying to Asia in high style. Luxurious berths in the aircraft cabin and Pan American hotels at each stop assured the ride wouldn't be rough.

BRIDGING THE GATE

CHIEF ENGINEER JOSEPH BAERMAN STRAUSS STOOD UP to his full 5 feet 3 inches on May 28 when President Franklin D. Roosevelt's telegraph key signal was relayed to San Francisco from Washington, D.C. It was a moment of truth for a bridge and a moment of less than the full truth for Strauss.

This was the day in 1937 when the brand new Golden Gate Bridge would be tested with vehicle traffic. The day before, on May 27, an estimated 200,000 people had walked about a mile north on the bridge from San Francisco to Marin County. Scoffers had called it "the bridge that couldn't be built." Well, they had been wrong. Roosevelt gave the signal, and the bridge was open!

Fire sirens and church bells began clanging. The two big ships just below the bridge started tooting their horns. The deep mournful drone of foghorns around the bay joined in. Four hundred planes did a flyover.

Strauss had been involved with the Golden Gate Bridge project for twenty years. A drawbridge designer, he had never formally

- 85 -

studied engineering. His well-respected Chicago bridge engineering firm had carried through with the project, despite political delays and questions about design, cost, and who was actually responsible for the bridge's innovative design. Strauss had insured that he'd personally have all the credit.

The remarkable suspension bridge was 1.7 miles long, with a 4,200-foot-long center span 220 feet above water that could rush through the strait from the Pacific Ocean into San Francisco Bay at 60 miles per hour. Each of the two art-deco-style towers thrust 746 feet above the water and 500 feet higher than the bridge roadway. Only eleven workers had died constructing a bridge that required 80,000 miles of steel wire be twined and strung between the towers and anchorages on both shores. Despite those unfortunate deaths, safety nets had prevented more fatalities in the notoriously chilly, churning waters below.

Workers were desperate for jobs during the Depression and were willing to climb towers for up to forty minutes before their paid working time began. Ironworkers and divers were in sudden demand. Above the water the men had to contend with howling winds, frequent fog, damp slippery surfaces, narrow catwalks, and iron smoothed to an icy slickness. Below, divers faced rough tidal currents, crashing waves, and the risk of decompression illness also known as the bends.

Strauss, the master persuader, later summed up his experience saying, "It took two decades and 200 million words to convince people that the bridge was feasible; then only four years and $35 million to put the concrete and steel together." They had also competed with the men who built the silver San Francisco-Oakland Bay Bridge between San Francisco, Yerba Buena Island, and Oakland in the East Bay that was completed in 1936.

The automobile created demand for faster transportation to San Francisco. Ferryboats carried passengers and 100,000 cars around the bay each year, but the pace was leisurely, not modern, complained critics. *San Francisco Bulletin* editor and Marin County resident, James Wilkins, had written in 1916 that it took too much time for workers to get to their jobs. Railroad tycoon Charles Crocker had proposed a bridge to span the Golden Gate in 1872, and even the crazy Emperor Norton had issued a proclamation in 1869 that called for a suspension bridge across the bay and out to the Farallon Islands 26 miles offshore.

Now the Golden Gate Bridge was built and painted a startling orange-red called International Orange. The color fit the name Golden Gate, though it had been Captain John C. Frémont who in 1846 had named the strait Chrysopylae, or Golden Gate, after the harbor entrance in Byzantium, or Istanbul. Strauss had fought against the U.S. Navy's plan to paint his bridge in black and yellow stripes—a hideous camouflage proposed in the event that warfare came to America's shores in the next few years.

Strauss hoped no one was reminded of his original plan that had proposed a heavy combination cantilever and suspension bridge. Strauss had never before built a bridge span longer than 300 feet. Consulting Engineer Leon Moisseiff, brought in as a famous suspension bridge expert, proposed an elegant, very long suspension bridge. Even the consulting architects Irving and Gertrude Morrow, who had their hands on the design, sketched towers without visible cross bracing that tapered as each rose into the sky, for a lighter effect and art deco look. To help secure his reputation, Strauss knew it helped that the bridge had been finished early and under budget.

Charles Alton Ellis, a University of Illinois structural and bridge engineering professor, had been part of the project as design engineer since 1922. Numbers were Ellis's specialty. He had spent four months running the numbers on every technical detail required by the Golden Gate Bridge design that he had roughed out with New York's Manhattan Bridge designer Moisseiff. He eventually handed Strauss his calculations. Ellis knew how much of what went where, but Strauss knew how to handle the politics and funding.

Strauss's personal secretary would later report that Strauss had handed out envelopes with $100 to San Francisco supervisors to help persuade them to go along with his plans. In salesman mode during the height of the Depression in 1932, Strauss approached the Bank of America's chief, A. P. Giannini. The banker, a San Franciscan who had loaned money to immigrants without collateral after the 1906 Earthquake, listened to Strauss's pitch and underwrote $6 million in bonds.

Strauss had already fired Ellis in 1931 after the Golden Gate Bridge District had approved Ellis's design with Strauss's name on it. Bridge construction began on January 5, 1933. Ellis continued to work on the bridge's structural design numbers and filled ten books, but was never paid for his extra efforts. Ellis and his successor, Clifford Paine, who was Strauss's assistant during construction, were both frozen out of recognition for their work.

Ellis's dismissal was complete, and Strauss insured that Ellis's name did not appear any place where credit could be given. Strauss's name was on the documents and plaques, but Ellis's co-workers, students, and admirers knew of Professor Ellis's accomplishments, and they made sure that Ellis's story and the full truth was told.

INTERNMENT DISPLACEMENT

- 1942 -

POINTING HER HEAVY CAMERA UP, Dorothea Lange captured the image of a Japanese man holding his overall-clad two-year-old son on his right arm. The man was San Francisco-born Dave Tatsuno who had graduated from the University of California in 1936, six years earlier. At 1625 Buchanan Street in Nihonmachi, San Francisco's Japantown, Tatsuno had paused while packing his possessions. He smiled for Lange, the famous Depression-era photographer from San Francisco, as he posed for her while reading his college notes.

Lange was on an assignment as a photographic investigator. She had been hired in early April 1942 by the local office of the War Relocation Authority. Her job was to document the evacuation and relocation of Japanese—both Japanese-American-born citizens and noncitizens of Japanese origin. The United States had been at war with Japan less than four months after the bombing of Pearl Harbor in Hawaii. Thousands of residents of Japanese heritage had been given notice that they were to move away from the Pacific Coast.

President Franklin D. Roosevelt issued Executive Order No. 9066 on February 19, giving the Secretary of War the authority to remove from militarily sensitive areas anyone deemed likely to engage in espionage or sabotage. On March 2 the Western Defense Command in San Francisco issued Proclamation No. 1, which ordered all people of Japanese ancestry to voluntarily leave the coastal areas. No such order was given for people of German and Italian background even though the United States was also at war with those European nations.

People from the western interior states reacted with hysteria against the Japanese and protested the proximity of 112,000 people who resided in the three coastal states "of Japanese ancestry" being moved near them. On March 27 suggested voluntary self-displacement ended. Japanese Americans were ordered to wait for supervised evacuation and were told they would be confined. The 93,000 people of Japanese ancestry in California, including 8,000 in San Francisco, did not have long to wait.

On April 13, Dave Tatsuno deliberately made time for Lange's photograph. He was the son of Japanese immigrant Shojiro Tatsuno, who had arrived from Nagano, Japan, in 1893. Shojiro opened a general store called Nichi Bei Bussan in Chinatown in 1902. Destroyed by the 1906 Earthquake and Fire, the Tatsuno business was rebuilt and eventually settled in Japantown at Post and Buchanan Streets in the 1920s. The shop's goods and clothing were American made.

Young Japanese men had come to San Francisco in the 1870s when the Meiji emperor opened Japan to Western ideas and encouraged students to study abroad. They settled into the existing Asian enclave of Chinatown, but associated mainly with other Japanese at social clubs, the YMCA, churches, and associations based on their Japanese regional origin. Other Japanese men arrived in the 1890s as contract laborers in fields, canneries, and mines. After Chinatown burned in 1906, the Japanese who remained in San Francisco, like Shojiro, moved west of the dynamited area of Van Ness Avenue and created Nihonmachi.

As Exclusion Acts barred or limited Chinese immigration, an incident over whether Japanese children could be forced to attend a segregated Chinese school built after the earthquake gave President Theodore Roosevelt an excuse to limit Japanese immigration. In return, Japan agreed not to issue passports to its laborers. A loophole in the system permitted matchmakers to arrange for the proxy marriage of Japanese women to Japanese men who were residents of the United States and who chose their imported "picture brides" from photographs. However, no Japanese-born person could become a naturalized citizen. Until 1942 it had been assumed that Japanese Americans born in the United States were citizens.

Lange was on the street in front of 2031 Bush Street as Japanese *issei* (immigrants) and *nisei* (first-generation born in the United States), dressed in their best clothes, lined up to register their household members for the mandatory evacuation. They did not know where they would be going, but they feared a prison or concentration camp. Nichi Ben Bussan's "Evacuation Sale" had sold almost everything at a low price. Dave Tatsuno's family was typical—permitted to pack only bedding and linens, toilet articles, extra clothing, and kitchen dishes and utensils.

The photographer documented the first of thousands of *issei, nisei,* and their children boarding U.S. Army buses in late April. Some Japanese waved and said they would be back soon. San Francisco Japanese were evacuated to Tanforan racetrack in San Bruno, just south of San Francisco. Undoubtedly, some had watched the famous horse, *Seabiscuit,* race there a few years before. Now the displaced were pointed to temporary housing in the stables.

West Coast Japanese evacuees were transferred to one of ten internment camps within a few months. Lange again photographed them boarding buses and drove out to the eastern Sierra Nevada internment camp in the cold, windy, raw, and desolate landscape of a place called Manzanar.

Dave Tatsuno's family was sent to Topaz, Utah. Tarpaper-covered barracks without plumbing or cooking facilities housed families of five or six in a single 20-foot by 25-foot room. They slept on Army cots, and each area had a small heating stove. One bath, toilet, and laundry building was shared by more than 250 people. Food was provided by the government, though in Topaz and the other camps, the Japanese raised their own crops whenever possible. They had basic medical treatment, ran their own schools and internal court, and worked at the rate of $16 per month for a forty-four-hour week. Guards scrutinized the barbed wire that surrounded the internment camp and manned its watchtowers.

Dave Tatsuno, who had enjoyed making home movies for years, somehow obtained an 8-millimeter camera and kept it hidden in a baby's shoebox. He carefully filmed movies of his family and daily life in the camp.

When Tatsuno and the other Japanese-Americans were released, they returned to find that their property, businesses, and farms had been sold off at low rates. Many had to start over, farming others' land or rebuilding businesses. San Francisco city officials had wasted no time declaring Nihonmachi a rat-infested and filthy slum and had set about demolishing the Japanese-American homes for redevelopment. Dave Tatsuno started a branch of Nichi Ben Bussan in San Jose, while his brother took over in the remnants of San Francisco's Nihonmachi.

In 1984 a United States court ruled that the act of internment of Japanese ancestry was racism and that the action was based on unsubstantiated facts and distortions. The Civil Rights Act of 1988 went further and compensated each internee or family $20,000 for loss of businesses or farms.

Dave Tatsuno never forgot. His home movie footage, *Topaz,* of life in the internment camp was placed in the Library of Congress National Film Registry in 1997.

THE BEATNIKS "HOWL"

- 1955 -

"I SAW THE BEST MINDS OF MY GENERATION destroyed by madness," intoned a little-known twenty-nine-year-old Jewish poet from New York named Allen Ginsberg.

The Six Gallery crowd, giddy after three hours of drinking cheap red wine, started to focus. A friend in the audience, probably Jack Kerouac, started shouting, "Go! Go! Go!" Soon everyone was chanting, "Go!" as Ginsberg continued through line after line, stanza after stanza of his unfinished poem, *Howl.*

The atmosphere was electric. The poem's sad, stark words were shocking. The sexually graphic paragraphs that followed the opening line of *Howl* were raw with emotion. Ginsberg verbalized the attitudes, fears, and disillusionment of his Beat Generation.

Jazz musicians used the slang word "beat" for someone who was broke or down on luck and living on the street. Beat philosophy was a weariness with life and bleak prospects for the future mixed with anger, Buddhist concepts, and even occasional humor.

Ginsberg, a writer and poet with some training in advertising, had organized this poetry reading of five men on October 7, 1955, at the experimental art gallery on Fillmore Street. Local bohemians, or beats as they called themselves, including the poets, had received Ginsberg's postcards advertising "a remarkable collection of angels on one stage reading their poetry . . . sharp, new, straightforward writing." About 150 poets attended the event along with friends of the poets and published poet Lawrence Ferlinghetti, who was the owner of the renowned City Lights Bookstore. Other hangers-on were smoking and drinking as they listened. The veteran anarchist and bohemian poet, Kenneth Rexroth, acted as master of ceremonies for the free event.

The beats were hard-living their bohemian existence in San Francisco, across the bay in Berkeley, or spending time going between the San Francisco Bay Area, New York, Mexico City, and Paris. Rent in San Francisco's North Beach was affordable, where transplanted New Yorker Ferlinghetti had the country's first paperback bookstore and City Lights publishing house. North Beach coffeehouses and bars were also cheap; the beats spent most of their days and nights there, talking philosophy, reading poetry, or listening to jazz. The hipsters came and went frequently, wrote poetry and books, discovered Buddhism, and experimented with drugs and sex.

> *I saw the best minds of my generation destroyed by*
> *madness, starving, hysterical, naked,*
> *dragging themselves through the negro streets at dawn*
> *looking for an angry fix,*
> *angelheaded hipsters burning for the ancient heavenly*
> *connection to the starry dynamo in the machinery of*
> *night, . . .*

Ginsberg had everyone's attention.

Optimism at the end of World War II had faded by the time many of the next decade's Beat Generation were attending college. Many feared an atomic bomb like those the United States dropped on Japan at Nagasaki and Hiroshima would be used again. And newsreels had shown the European concentration camps where millions of Jews had been exterminated.

By 1948 the Soviet Union's spreading influence in eastern Europe sparked the Cold War and the Iron Curtain that separated communism from capitalism. In the early 1950s the United States fought against communism in Korea. Soon the U.S. Senate was holding hearings on people's membership in the Communist party, which was considered treason.

At home in the American South, racial tension was high. In 1954 the U.S. Supreme Court had ruled against racially segregated schools. Incidents flared, including the murder in Mississippi of fourteen-year-old African-American Emmett Till.

The Beat Generation reacted to the turmoil of the '50s. Ginsberg, the son of a well-known poet and teacher, didn't always attend his Columbia University classes, choosing instead to live like a homeless person on the New York streets. From that perspective affluence seemed remote and unattainable. Ginsberg had personally experienced what it was like to be homeless and destitute, an anguished mood he evoked when reading *Howl* in San Francisco that day in 1955.

Surrealist poet Philip Lamantia had kicked off the evening at 8:00 P.M. by reading the work of a poet friend who had died of a peyote overdose. Jack Kerouac, who would publish *The Dharma Bums* and *On the Road* within a few years, declined to read his poetry in favor of taking up a collection for wine. Twenty-two-year-old Kansan Michael McClure read his poem about the machine gun slaying of one hundred killer whales by U.S. soldiers. Oregonian Philip

Whalen's poem described the alienation many beats felt. Then Ginsberg read:

> *. . . with the absolute heart of the poem of life butchered*
> *out of their own bodies good to eat a thousand years.*

The audience applauded as Ginsberg, weeping, ended his poem of 36,000 words. Poet Gary Snyder read last.

By the next morning, five new young poets, especially Ginsberg, were acclaimed as celebrities. The beats, who preferred berets and black clothes, had gone out to eat and drink after the reading, but without Ferlinghetti, who they considered a bookstore owner, not a poet.

Ferlinghetti later sent a telegram to Ginsberg using words Ralph Waldo Emerson had sent in a letter to one of Ginsberg's heroes, Walt Whitman: "I greet you at the beginning of a great career. When do I get the manuscript?" Ginsberg gave many more public readings of *Howl* in San Francisco and Berkeley for larger and larger audiences. Months later *Howl* was ready for City Lights Pocket Poets publication as *Howl and Other Poems*.

Publisher Ferlinghetti had hired an English printer to produce the paperback, but the copies were initially impounded and prevented from entering the United States by the customs department. The books were released, but then the San Francisco police department filed suit against Ferlinghetti to prevent the publication from being distributed; they declared that *Howl's* language and blunt descriptions of gay sex were obscene.

On September 9, 1957, almost two years after the reading at Six Gallery and with Ginsberg far away in Paris, *Howl* was protected under the First Amendment. Judge Clayton W. Horn ruled that *Howl* possessed redeeming social importance, vindicating

Ferlinghetti and the American Civil Liberties Union that had defended his right to publish *Howl*.

What no beat could have guessed when the obscenity ruling on *Howl* was issued was that within the month the Soviet Union would launch *Sputnik*, the first man-made earth-orbiting satellite. The press couldn't resist: The beats became "beatniks."

UN-AMERICAN HOSING

-1960 -

Are you now or have you ever been a member of the Communist Party?

STUDENTS AT THE UNIVERSITY OF CALIFORNIA, BERKELEY, and other protesters who had wanted to enter the hearing room on May 13 were gone, washed down the curving marble staircase of the San Francisco City Hall rotunda. Water blasts from high-powered hoses normally used to fight fires had been aimed directly at seated demonstrators. City fathers—or at least the man in charge, Police Inspector Michael McGuire—were taking no chances that the hearings for the U.S. House Un-American Activities Committee, HUAC, in San Francisco from May 12 to 14 in 1960, would be disrupted.

Since the early 1950s the FBI had gathered information on teachers who, FBI director J. Edgar Hoover had decided, might be teaching Communism in schools. Schools included the University of California where all employees had been required to sign loyalty oaths since 1949. The FBI provided the University of California and other schools with names of alleged Communists and sympathizers. During the 1950s some University of California professors had been fired for refusing to sign the loyalty oath.

HUAC had been in San Francisco in 1953, 1956, and 1957. Now it was back. One-quarter of its subpoenaed witnesses were teachers, and one UC Berkeley student had also been summoned.

Are you now or have you ever been a member of the Communist Party?

The question hung in the air inside the Board of Supervisors' hearing room in San Francisco's City Hall. The scuffling, yelling, singing, and noise that had been going on outside the second floor hearing room doors had suddenly ceased a short time before.

Bill Mandel, the subpoenaed witness, paused. He had sent his 15-year-old son out of the hearing a short time before. The spectators packed into the closed room strained to hear his answer.

HUAC had been trying to identify Communists around the nation since the late 1940s. In 1947 Hollywood actors and writers had been named alleged Communists by studio heads and others. They appeared under HUAC subpoena in Washington, D.C. Ten entertainment industry witnesses cited the First Amendment of the U.S. Constitution as a reason not to answer the question regarding Communist membership. An affirmative answer could mean treason, while "no" indicated loyalty to the United States.

Those ten and others who reluctantly followed in the witness chair and refused to answer were blacklisted and thus unable to find work. Some like author and screenwriter, Dalton Trumbo, used other names in order to get work. Trumbo's *Roman Holiday* script won an Oscar at the 1953 Academy Awards under someone else's name.

From 1950 to 1954 Senator Joseph "Joe" McCarthy had used the committee to denounce supposed Communists and those who sympathized with the Cold War enemy of the United States—the Soviet Union. People all over the country were asked to "name names" of Communists, and some did. Those named were subpoenaed, and some of them revealed other names even if they had no connection to Communist activity.

Staff corruption and an attempted cover-up brought McCarthy down in late 1954 when the U.S. Senate condemned him for "conduct contrary to senatorial traditions." But HUAC and its aura of suspicion survived with the support of what committee members and others were told was incriminating information in FBI files.

In the late 1950s some students at the University of California, Berkeley, identified the racial discrimination practiced by sororities and fraternities as an issue to protest. Their protest efforts were organized as SLATE, a term named after the issues platform on which a group of candidates ran for student office. SLATE was branded a political party instead of a student organization of the university, and it was eventually ordered off the Berkeley campus.

With HUAC's announced reappearance in May 1960, SLATE members decided to protest the singling out of their professors and a student for questioning about loyalty. In late April SLATE members and others formed Students of Civil Liberties. The new group's petition to have HUAC abolished had 2,000 signatures inscribed within four days. A rally at San Francisco's Union Square was planned for May 12. Afterwards some students tried to get into the City Hall hearing room, but passes were mostly given to people known and approved by HUAC. As a result some scuffling occurred inside the HUAC hearing room.

On Friday, May 13, students and other demonstrators lined up for hearing passes, but the white admission cards were again handed to HUAC-approved spectators. The protestors pushed against police barricades that protected the hearing room entrance, and the police pushed the barricade back. Protest organizers got the crowd singing and directed people to sit down.

Eventually the barricade push had become too much. Police Inspector McGuire opened the fire hydrants, and scuffling and screaming began as protesters were shoved back and down by the force of water pressure. Through the wet and commotion, stick-wielding San Francisco police arrested sixty-eight people.

Inside the hearing room Mandel heard about the happenings outside. After he heard that his son was safe, he began to speak:

> *I want the fullest glare of publicity on this committee's activities . . . men who sit there in violation of the United States Constitution . . . a kangaroo court. It does not have my respect, it has my utmost contempt.*

Mandel's words and the police action against student protestors and others shocked San Franciscans. An estimated 5,000 people protested at City Hall on the last day of the HUAC hearings.

Charges against sixty-seven protesters were dropped quickly, and the remaining man was acquitted within a year. The protest movement that was to use the sit-down as a tactic during the Free Speech Movement on the Berkeley campus in 1964 coalesced in 1960 when a cascade of water swept nonviolent protesters down the San Francisco City Hall steps.

HUAC hearings never returned to San Francisco. The committee changed its name to the House Internal Security Committee in 1969 and was abolished in 1975.

H'ASHBURY LOV'IN

- 1967 -

DR. TIMOTHY LEARY WAS IN HIS ELEMENT in front of the crowd of 20,000 or so people gathered in Golden Gate Park on a sunny January afternoon in 1967. "Turn on, tune in, drop out," the one-time Harvard professor and current LSD guru intoned into the microphone.

People elsewhere in the United States on January 14 were beginning to worry about the ever-escalating Vietnam War. Sports fans were anticipating midwinter distraction: A new football championship game called the Super Bowl was to be played the next day. In San Francisco, though, the counterculture was out in force. The milling throng brought together from across the bay in Berkeley both radical student activists and peace advocates determined to resist the war effort. Most of them were white and under thirty.

The HUMAN BE-IN poster's rainbow colors had been hard to miss during the past few weeks in storefront windows along Haight Street. The Human Be-In was destined to put "the Haight," or the

"Hashbury"—as it was sometimes called after the hashish enjoyed by many denizens—on the international map.

The Haight-Ashbury was named for the intersection of the two streets in the heart of a rundown district close to Golden Gate Park. It was a center for counterculture in Northern California. Neighborhood Victorian houses had seen better days, but the large spacious flats were cheap, and landlords were not too fussy about the number of inhabitants. Up the Mount Parnassus hill was the University of California, San Francisco, medical school where post doctorate fellow Dr. David Smith was injecting lab rats with LSD (Lysergic Acid Diethylamide). All he had to do was wander down to the Haight near Golden Gate Park's eastern panhandle and see young people high on the same psychedelic drug. He was worried.

The poster, with bright green shading into blue, had urged BRING FLOWERS, INCENSE, FEATHERS, CANDLES, BANNERS, FLAGS. The pungent scent of patchouli oil overlay the sweet odor of incense from India that wafted from shop doorways where the posters were stacked for the taking.

A GATHERING OF THE TRIBES . . . BRING FAMILIES,
ANIMALS, CYMBALS, DRUMS, CHIMES, FLUTES . . . ALL
OF SAN FRANCISCO'S ROCK BANDS INCLUDING SANTANA
AND THE STEVE MILLER BAND

Allen Ginsberg, the beat whose poem *Howl* had sparked an obscenity trial a decade before, was dressed in white near some trees, chanting, dancing, and waving his arms. Some of the hippies, as *San Francisco Chronicle* columnist Herb Caen had named them, were dancing, chanting, smoking marijuana, or taking other drugs.

San Francisco's prolific rock bands played frequent gigs at the Fillmore Auditorium and Avalon Ballroom. The light shows added visual effects to the psychedelic-inspired music—pulsing strobes and amoeba-like colors flashed and oozed around the walls and ceilings. The Jefferson Airplane and the Grateful Dead lived nearby in the Haight and were among the top-name performers at the Human Be-In. Yet even with all the rock bands out in force, The Human Be-In begun simply with the sound of a single conch shell.

The man behind the poster and the Human Be-In was poet Alan Cohen. *The Oracle,* with a prism of colors on its cover, was based on a Cohen vision. The tabloid newspaper debuted in September 1966 and contained counterculture writing and art. LSD became illegal in California in October. By January 1967 Bay Area hippies were grabbing *The Oracle* and rock concert posters with psychedelic swirls and bold writhing letters as soon as they rolled off the presses.

The first Human Be-In received significant international press coverage, which described the event as a mixture of meditation, chants, silence, pounding rock music, drugs, partying, flowers, and dancing. Similarly the media amply covered a one-hundred-person-strong Vietnam War protest march from Second and Market Streets to the edge of Golden Gate Park on April 15.

People were talking about an upcoming June music concert in Monterey, 100 miles south of San Francisco. To promote the Monterey Pop Festival, John Phillips of The Mamas and the Papas wrote, "San Francisco (Be Sure to Wear Some Flowers in Your Hair)." Scott McKenzie's version of the song hit the airwaves in May 1967 with the seductive refrain, "summertime will be a love-in there." Thousands of people headed to San Francisco and its cheap, psychedelic mecca, the Haight-Ashbury.

The 200,000 young people who descended on San Francisco called it the Summer of Love. Some camped in Golden Gate Park. Others found a place to sleep—a crash pad—in crowded apartments or communes. A group called The Diggers asked for donations of food from local merchants and fed the masses for free. The Mime Troupe, a protest theatre group, performed in the Panhandle of Golden Gate Park, and some street musicians played for a place to crash for the night or for marijuana and LSD, which were often handed out for free on the streets.

Smith, or "Dr. Dave" as the Haight-Ashbury regulars called him, found that youngsters on the streets were taking drugs and contacting sexually transmitted diseases. He went to San Francisco city officials to intervene. When they did not, he used funds from a lecture and a neighborhood church to set up a small office and recruit volunteers to help out for the summer at what he called the Haight Ashbury Free Medical Clinic. Rock bands played benefits, and rock concert impresario Bill Graham made sure that Dr. Dave had enough supplies to help his patients.

Summer turned into fall, and Dr. Dave started to see more victims of violence and fewer Flower Children, which was the name given to San Francisco's Summer of Love hippies. The wave of peaceable, drug-happy youth started packing up onto hippie buses or moving to rural areas. The Summer of Love was brief.

Dr. Dave and his unpaid staff continued to treat hundreds of patients who were under the influence of drugs, or sick in the mind, body, or both. Over the years his free medical clinic became the model for 300 free clinics around the United States, and his urgent care team of musicians set the standard for giving benefit concerts for emergency treatment. The Haight Ashbury Free Clinics, Inc., with a handful of paid doctors and many volunteers, is still on Haight Street.

The Haight-Ashbury remained a magnet for young people and others drawn by the aura of free drugs, sex, and an easy-going lifestyle. For the next few years the rest of the city was absorbed with peace marches against the Vietnam War. In 1969 hundreds of thousands flocked to antiwar rallies at the Polo Field in Golden Gate Park and grooved along with protest songs from some of the same rock groups that had been singing more mellow tunes just two years before during the Summer of Love.

LA RAZA RISING

- 1968 -

"On Strike! Shut it down!" The marching San Francisco State College students were angry. Some students hurried on to classes, trying to avoid the commotion. Others paused to see what the day's adrenaline rush was going to be.

It was November 6, 1968, toward the end of a year that had seen turmoil in the streets of Paris and Mexico City as well as closer to home on California high school and college campuses.

The chanting got louder as students approached the administration building. Leaders of the Black Students Union and Third World Liberation Front (TWLF) wanted a black teacher, who was also the Black Panther Party Minister of Education, reinstated. The TWLF, a coalition of the Black Students Union, Filipino Americans, Latin-American students, and Mexican-American students' El Renacimiento, was also demanding an Ethnic Studies School.

Rupert García had been listening to what fellow Mexican Americans and other students were saying about their sense of unique cultural identity and the need for action against injustice. Mexican Americans born in the United States had begun to call themselves Chicanos to distinguish themselves from people born in Mexico. Like many Chicanos in California, García had been born and raised in the state's Central Valley, physically and economically apart from white society.

The twenty-seven-year-old painter had started studying art at San Francisco State College in 1966 after he returned from four years of military service. He had spent his last year in the U.S. Air Force at a secret northern Thailand base as American military operations in Vietnam escalated. Before returning home, García had heard there was an antiwar movement and decided it was wise to keep quiet about his service.

Mexican Americans had become identified in the press with César Chávez, who had organized the National Agricultural Workers Union in 1962. In 1965 Chávez's union had joined Filipino grape pickers in a strike against Central Valley grape growers. In 1968 Chávez, a believer in nonviolent protest, had fasted for twenty-five days as his union started a California grape boycott.

The whole world was watching ethnic civil rights movements, the Vietnam conflict, and American presidential politics in 1968. In late January during the Tet Lunar New Year, the Vietnamese National Liberation Front attacked South Vietnamese cities and U.S. troops. On April 4 the Memphis assassination of Dr. Martin Luther King Jr. triggered race riots around the United States and horrified the nation, including art student Rupert García. Moreover, Robert F. Kennedy was assassinated in Los Angeles in early June after winning the California Democratic Party presidential primary. By late August demonstrators were chanting, "The Whole World is Watching," as Chicago police beat antiwar protesters outside the Democratic Party Convention.

Back on campuses in fall 1968, students were ready to protest the Vietnam War buildup and the lack of attention to ethnic minority studies. García and other ethnic political activists met in San Francisco. He learned about the civil rights movements for African Americans, Chicanos, Latinos, Asian Americans, and Native Americans and was aware of the views of Black Panthers, Marxists, and Trotskyites. Years later for a Smithsonian Institution interviewer, García recalled: "I began to see this global interconnection of these movements of protest and critique and a desire to redesign the fabric of society, to define and produce a new human being." The ex-soldier had become politicized.

A teacher who had returned from France told art students at San Francisco State that he had seen French students making effective protest posters. García along with other art students and professors formed a "poster brigade." For the time being García stopped painting, and he and other artists taught themselves to silkscreen posters protesting racism, the Vietnam War, and police violence. Che Guevara pictured above the caption, "¡Right On!" was one of García's most recognized poster designs.

García's poster art was ready for the Black Students Union and TWLF protest on November 6. What protesters would not know was that the march scheduled for that day at the San Francisco State College administration building was the beginning of months of turmoil. Student and teacher strikes continued for four and a half months. García and other art students reorganized their classes to make the curricula meaningful.

As 1969 dawned, 350 members of the American Federation of Teachers went on strike at San Francisco State for educational reforms, a work contract, police withdrawal from campus, and agreement with student demands. By March 20 the demands had been

met, and the strikes were over. By the next term García was a gradu-
ate student teacher in the new La Raza Studies program teaching historic and ethnic studies for Mexican Americans and Hispanics.
Another Latino artist invited García to visit Artes Seis (Six Arts)
gallery in San Francisco's Mission District. García was impressed with
the Latino artists' gallery in the heavily Hispanic neighborhood and
agreed to join the artists by teaching silk screening to the community.
It was art mixed with discussions of politics and ethnicity. To empha-
size his support of Latino art in the Mission District, García's gradu-
ate degree art exhibit was at Artes Seis.

In 1970 García and other Latino artists moved Artes Seis to
Fourteenth and Valencia Streets and changed its name to Galería de
la Raza, or The People's Gallery, to include not only the Chicanos
but also the Latinos in the neighborhood. Latino writers and poets
were publishing political commentaries and poetry while musicians
like Carlos Santana were frequent visitors to the Mission District.
"We saw ourselves as paralleling and crisscrossing with the social
and political thrust of the moment," remembered García, who
began painting again after having devoted seven years exclusively to
creating protest posters.

Galería de la Raza has expanded its exhibits to include digital
murals, bringing online the themes, bright colors, politics, and emo-
tions of murals on the walls and garage doors of Mission District
streets. Balmy Alley's collection of more than twenty murals was organized as a group effort in 1972. Several hundred of the Mission District's
murals have come and gone over the years, but many have been
restored more than once and remain as La Raza's cultural treasures.

INVASION OF ALCATRAZ

- 1969 -

"MAYDAY! MAYDAY! THE INDIANS HAVE LANDED!" Glenn Dodson, Alcatraz Island's caretaker and sole defender alerted authorities on the mainland in San Francisco, a little over a mile away across San Francisco Bay. Alcatraz Island was being invaded at 2:00 A.M.; it wasn't under attack, and no shots were fired, but Dodson had been roused from sleep by the ruckus.

The caretaker heard cheering from Alcatraz's eastern shoreline early on this clear November 20, 1969, morning. He hurried to where seventy-nine Indians, including six children, were making triumphal noise as they landed on "The Rock." A Native-American invasion of Alcatraz by more than twenty tribes had begun.

Treacherous tides and chilly water between Alcatraz and the city had prevented most of the 1,554 occupants from escaping from Alcatraz Federal Penitentiary between 1934 and 1963. Five escapees disappeared forever—adding to the reputation of the prison's "incorrigibles" who were subject to occasional isolation and solitary confinement. Prisoners had included gangster Al Capone and Robert Stroud, whom everybody called The Birdman of Alcatraz.

Spaniard Juan Manuel de Ayala had named the island, *isla alcatraces,* Pelican Island, when he sailed into San Francisco Bay in 1775. The rocky, almost barren surface was favored by nesting birds. By the mid-1850s the U.S. Army had taken over to defend the growing city of San Francisco and the new State of California, and the lighthouse kept ships from disastrous wrecks. During the Civil War Alcatraz was armed with cannons and eventually held imprisoned Army deserters. Native American Hopis were incarcerated on the island after being captured in Arizona's late-nineteenth-century Indian Wars. In 1898 Spanish-American War prisoners arrived.

The U.S. Army and, later, the Bureau of Prisons faced saltwater-corroded plumbing and the high cost of transporting all supplies by boat, including water, food, clothing, heating fuel, and building materials. Guards' children had to take a ferry to school in San Francisco, and even the warden's wife's flower garden required constant tending. Heavy fog, damp climate, and wind blowing eastward through the Golden Gate made the isolated island stark.

In 1964 the U.S. government's General Services Administration declared Alcatraz up for auction. In March Sioux took over the island for a few hours, claiming it as surplus federal land based on an 1868 Indian treaty. Eventually San Francisco Mayor Joseph Alioto accepted Texas oilman Lamar Hunt's proposal to level Alcatraz's buildings and build a casino on the island, but not everyone agreed. In 1969 a national park to protect San Francisco's beach, shore, and bay parks was proposed by the Department of the Interior. Officials considered whether Alcatraz should be included.

During the 1960s the Free Speech and Civil Rights movements, United Farmworkers Union strikes by Hispanic farmworkers, and marches against the Vietnam War had created social and political activism among students, ethnic minorities, and the economically deprived.

In the 1950s many Native Americans had been removed from their designated reservations by government policy that claimed rights to mineral, water, and land-based resources. Thousands thronged to the cities, including San Francisco. Indian household income averaged $1,500 per year, and the Native-Americans' life expectancy was only about forty-four years. Indian activists went on the offensive. They declared, "Alcatraz is an island," land no one valued that would replace some of their land surrendered by treaty.

On November 9, 1969, Indians gathered at San Francisco's Pier 39 to go to Alcatraz. When boats didn't arrive, Richard Oakes read the *Indians of All Nations: The Proclamation to the Great White Father* [President Richard Nixon] *and his People.* Oakes and his fellow Native Americans claimed the crumbling Alcatraz facilities with a treaty offering $24 in glass beads and cloths like those that had bought Manhattan for the Dutch centuries before. The declaration created a Bureau of Caucasian Affairs, which ironically paralleled the Bureau of Indian Affairs that was perceived to be nonresponsive to Indian needs and claims. The Indians of All Nations would, Oakes read, create on Alcatraz a Native American Studies center, spiritual center, trades and crafts training center, an environmental studies school, and a cultural history museum.

Eventually seventy-five Indians boarded a boat captained by a Canadian and symbolically circled Alcatraz. As the boat approached the island, Oakes led others by diving into the bay and started swimming to the island. The U.S. Coast Guard pulled them from the water. That evening fourteen activists did make it to the island and stayed overnight. The next morning the Coast Guard ended the attempted takeover.

However, the early morning landing of seventy-nine Indians on

November 20 played out differently. Caretaker Dodson declared himself one-eighth Indian and pointed the Native American invaders to the former warden's residence for shelter.

In the days that followed, the invaders were joined by a constantly changing group of Native Americans who defied a Coast Guard blockade to join the protesters for a few hours or many months at a time. There was drumming and chanting, arguing about their goals, and teaching Native American stories, dances, and crafts to the children. They lived in the former warden's house, prison facilities, and cellblocks. Cooking in the prison kitchen summoned ghosts, some thought, so most cooking was done outside. Children roamed about the crumbling cement buildings, and one died in a fall. John Trudell broadcast from Radio Free Alcatraz, and supporters from across the country and San Francisco sent clothing, food, and other supplies by boat.

Negotiations with the U.S. government for funds to build the proposed Indian centers, school, and museum were ongoing, but no agreement or treaty was created.

For the mix of reservation Indians, urbanized city-dwelling Native Americans, students, children, and tribal activists, there was endless disagreement over how to improve conditions. Strong personalities and disagreement about strategy frustrated many of the 5,600 Native Americans who visited Alcatraz during the occupation. Activists began to leave the island.

The Alcatraz lighthouse beacon extinguished during the occupation may have led to an oil spill in the bay, infuriating San Franciscans. When mysterious fires burned down many of the remaining noncellblock buildings, the invaders lost their remaining support.

The invasion that became an occupation lasted nineteen months. U.S. Marshals and FBI agents took the last fifteen Indians, including five children, peacefully from Alcatraz on June 11, 1971.

SUNSET BANK ROBBER

- 1974 -

THE "FBI WANTED" POSTER was blunt: NATIONAL FIREARMS ACT. MATERIAL WITNESS, it said in bold print under the mug shot of Patty Hearst. Heiress Patricia Campbell Hearst, who disliked being called Patty, was an FBI suspect in 1974. Her comfortable life as one of the granddaughters and heirs of newspaper magnate William Randolph Hearst would never be the same. She was only nineteen, holding a weapon in a bank, when all hell broke loose.

Two months earlier she had been an art history major at the University of California, Berkeley, living in an off-campus apartment. Though the campus had been politically active in the 1960s with the birth of the Free Speech Movement and protests against the Vietnam War, Patricia Hearst had never been involved with any political activities. Already engaged to be married, Hearst envisioned herself eventually working in a museum.

On February 4 Patty had been kidnapped from her apartment. She later remembered people being beaten, gunshots, and then two

African-American men and a white woman dragging her out of her residence. Members of a group called the Symbionese Liberation Army, or SLA, had grabbed her. Later police analysis showed cyanide-laced bullets had been fired into her apartment wall.

For twelve hours there was no media coverage of the apparent kidnapping of Patty Hearst, the only child of *San Francisco Examiner* president and editor Randolph Hearst. Then details on the SLA were reported.

The SLA's symbol was a seven-headed cobra, a reference to the symbiosis that gave the group its name. Some of the members were believed to have committed other crimes in Northern California.

The SLA took Patty to a house and confined her in a closet. For the next two months, she later said, she was brainwashed while gagged, blindfolded, bound, and sexually attacked.

Taped SLA demands were not for money but that food be given to the poor for free and that the group's ideological message be published. The Hearst family complied. However, the food distribution system didn't guarantee that food would get to the poor, and some food was resold by others. Patty wasn't freed.

The SLA also distributed tapes with Patty Hearst's voice saying she agreed with SLA ideas. Her parents received a photo of Patty holding a carbine in front of a flag with the SLA's cobra logo. Soon after another tape arrived announcing Patty as Tania, the name of the girlfriend of the late revolutionary Che Guevara.

In the bank's security videotape that captured her image on April 15, Patty Hearst looked thin and very different from the relaxed student she had been at Berkeley. April 15 was the day income tax returns were due, and banks would be busy with customers. The western residential districts of San Francisco were no exception, and the Hibernia Bank's Sunset District branch had a number of customers.

At 9:40 A.M., the five SLA bank robbers struck, yelling obscenities at people inside to get face down on the floor. A young woman with dark hair wearing a coat and beret held a carbine at the ready. Her face was clearly visible. Within four minutes the group got away with $10,000 and hurt two people in the process. Police investigating the incident recognized the gun-toting, beret-wearer as the missing heiress. Suddenly San Francisco was reading all about the latest SLA tapes, the food distributions made in response, and the confusion surrounding Patty's alliances.

Two days after the Hibernia Bank robbery, another tape stated that her gun had been loaded and "at no time did any of my comrades point their guns at me." Hearst denied being brainwashed as a ridiculous idea and said in the rhetoric of the time, "I am a soldier of the people's army."

During the next year and a half, Hearst was a fugitive from the law and the FBI. She fired warning shots to cover other SLA members who were shoplifting in Los Angeles and fled to safehouses after some SLA members died in a standoff with Los Angeles police on May 17. Her flight took her and another SLA couple to Pennsylvania, New York, and back to the Sacramento area. Cars were stolen and more banks robbed. Patty—as Tania—was believed to be involved.

Finally, on September 18, 1975, Hearst along with two other SLA members was arrested in a nondescript house in southern San Francisco, ironically only 3.3 miles from the bank branch she had robbed the year before. She was charged with armed bank robbery and use of a firearm to commit a felony at the Hibernia Bank. Her picture after the arrest shows a raised fist. When booked for the crimes she gave her occupation as "urban guerrilla."

Americans, along with San Franciscans close to where the robbery had occurred, debated whether Patty Hearst was a true believer in the SLA cause or had been brainwashed, as she maintained at trial. On

March 20, 1976, she was found guilty and sentenced to serve twenty-five years for robbery and ten years for firearms possession. The judge reduced the sentence, and Hearst ultimately spent twenty-one months in the Federal Correctional Institute in Pleasanton, California.

The photo of Patty Hearst holding a gun in front of the SLA banner became a symbol of the 1970s. Had she been brainwashed as she maintained? Or, had she been abused into believing in a terrorist cause that seemed opposite of her background?

In 1979 President Jimmy Carter commuted her sentence, and Hearst was released from prison. Patty Hearst went on to marry her bodyguard two months after her release from jail and raised her family in Connecticut. She later became a film actress, though not in documentaries made about her SLA period. She even wrote an auto-biography in 1982, *Every Secret Thing*.

As one of his last acts in office in 2001, President Bill Clinton granted Hearst a pardon. No one knows if Patricia "Patty" Hearst Shaw has ever returned to the Sunset District looking for the Hibernia Bank branch where her life changed forever. She won't find the bank, but for years she could have rented one of her films at the Hollywood Video store that occupied the spot at 1450 Noriega Street.

MURDER AT CITY HALL

- 1978 -

"Both Mayor Moscone and Supervisor Milk have been shot and killed," announced San Francisco's new mayor, Dianne Feinstein, her voice unsteady. The gasps of the reporters and City Hall staffers turned into horrified screams. Supervisor Feinstein, who had just succeeded George Moscone as mayor, continued slowly, "The suspect is Dan White."

Former Supervisor Dan White had been up all night, drinking Coke and eating Hostess Twinkies. He had recently resigned as a San Francisco supervisor, but with conservative supporters urging him to reconsider, White decided he wanted his old job back. The previous evening, November 26, 1978, a radio reporter called and told White she had heard that he wasn't going to work again at City Hall and asked for his reaction. White hung up on her.

The thirty-two-year-old White was born in San Francisco and had been a high school sports star; his former careers included Vietnam paratrooper, fireman, and policeman. He had given his resignation to

Mayor George Moscone, whose duty it would be to appoint someone in White's place. White said that the $9,600 supervisor salary wasn't enough to support his family, and as a supervisor he could not legally hold another job. His Pier 39 family-run fast food business wasn't doing well. White had campaigned hard on behalf of a statewide initiative to ban homosexuals as public school teachers. The measure had been defeated in the November election a few weeks before.

Moscone had accepted White's resignation. The liberal mayor and the other supervisors, including Harvey Milk, the first openly gay elected official from a major American city, knew that if Moscone appointed a liberal to replace the conservative White, the balance on the Board of Supervisors would tilt in the liberals' direction.

Milk and White had been elected in 1977, but the supervisors opposed each other on most issues. When White asked Mayor Moscone to reappoint him as supervisor, Milk had strongly urged Moscone to appoint someone else.

Harvey Milk represented the Castro District, a notably sunny area in central San Francisco where most residents were homosexual. In the 1970s gays and lesbians had started moving into the neighborhood's Victorian flats and patronized gay bars and shops. Milk's camera store on Castro Street was at ground central in San Francisco's gay community.

Milk was originally from New York, served in the U.S. Navy, campaigned for Barry Goldwater, and had been a stockbroker. By the time the forty-two-year-old Milk arrived in San Francisco in 1972, he had a ponytail and a hippie style, and he passionately believed in social reform. Milk, as a politician, cut his hair and dressed conservatively in a suit, but his ideas remained liberal and supportive of his gay community.

Milk called himself the unofficial mayor of Castro Street. He organized labor boycotts and a Castro District merchants' association while advocating gay representation in city government. He frequently walked along Castro Street with crowds of neighborhood residents following behind him, a charismatic, smiling man who seemed to know everyone's life histories and lifestyles. Milk ran for supervisor several times, always talking about hope and progress.

In 1976 Milk estimated that 130,000 residents—20 percent of San Francisco's population—were gay and that 20 percent of those lived in the Castro District. After several tries, he had been elected in 1977 to represent the Castro, in the city's first district, instead of city-wide, supervisor's race.

George Moscone had served on the Board of Supervisors in the 1960s before serving in the California Senate. Progressive Democrats Moscone and Assemblyman Willie Brown (who would become San Francisco mayor years later) had successfully carried a bill that outlawed California's sodomy laws. Milk's constituency approved and had supported Moscone when he successfully ran for mayor in 1975.

During sessions in the elegant, oak-paneled Board of Supervisors chambers, another newly elected supervisor, Carol Ruth Silver, sat between philosophical opponents Milk and White. Milk voted for a proposed psychiatric home in White's district that White opposed. White then cast the only vote against a gay rights law that was passed by the Board of Supervisors. The men clearly did not get along.

White arranged to have an assistant drive him to City Hall on the morning of November 27. He shaved, dressed, and made sure his police .38 Smith and Wesson was loaded and secured out of sight in its holster. He also took extra bullets.

At 10:15 A.M. White's assistant drove him to City Hall, where he requested to see both Moscone and Milk to ask why he wouldn't be reappointed as supervisor. As his assistant parked the car, White avoided a City Hall metal detector by going through a ground floor window. He went directly to the mayor's office and waited nervously as Moscone's secretary told the mayor that White was waiting. After a few minutes with Moscone, the secretary heard White shouting. A few minutes later, she heard four dull thuds. Only later would she know that White had fired at Moscone four times at close range and killed the mayor in an inner private office area.

White quickly left and headed toward Milk's office. Milk took him to White's former office. White had his revolver ready with hollow-point bullets that would explode on contact and then fired at Milk. By 10:55 A.M. Milk was dead.

This is Harvey Milk, speaking on Friday, November 18, 1977. This is to be played only in the event of my death by assassination . . . I fully realize that a person who stands for what I stand for, an activist, a gay activist, becomes the target or potential target for a person who is insecure, terrified, afraid, or very disturbed with themselves. . . . May the bullets that smash through my brain smash through every closet door in the nation . . .

Within a few hours of the City Hall murders, Milk's friends had gathered to hear a tape recording they knew existed but had never heard. Milk was determined to name a gay political successor if he was removed from the scene.

Dan White fled the murder scene and headed for a church before he found a policeman to whom he could confess to the murders and surrender. That night 40,000 silent marchers walked with lighted candles from Eighteenth and Castro Streets to City Hall at the Civic Center Plaza. Folk singer Joan Baez sang "Swing Low, Sweet Chariot."

White's defense attorneys summoned an expert witness. The psychiatrist testified that White's consumption of junk food the night before the murders was opposite his normal health-conscious eating habits and a sign of depression.

On May 21, 1979, a jury found Dan White guilty of voluntary manslaughter, not murder, based on what came to be called the "Twinkie defense." Dan White was sentenced to eight years in prison.

An angry crowd assembled in the Castro District and again marched to City Hall, gathering supporters as it went. This time the marchers weren't silent. Some broke City Hall windows and others started fires. Outside the buildings police cars were set ablaze, and some of the outraged marchers fought with police. People who returned to the Castro District noticed that Market Street business windows were broken.

Later that night San Francisco Police in riot gear formed a line at Eighteenth and Castro Streets and walked toward the crowd. The police entered the Elephant Walk, a popular gay bar, and began swinging sticks. Furniture was smashed and a riot later named the White Night Riot was on.

Dan White was already in Soledad State Prison where he would be confined for four years until he was paroled. Two years after his release, the one-time supervisor sat in his car listening to a sad Irish ballad and breathed his last breath of carbon monoxide from the car exhaust.

PARROTS ON TELEGRAPH HILL

- 1990 -

Like so many San Franciscans, the original parrots of Telegraph Hill were transplants from somewhere else. Mark Bittner was living in a cottage on Telegraph Hill when he spotted a particular group of feathered immigrants and wanted to know more. Bittner himself had immigrated to San Francisco from Seattle twenty years before. He acknowledged himself as a failed musician, occasional street person, and hopeful writer given to meditating. His three goals in life were to find a girlfriend (who would accept him even with long hair), work he loved, and a country place. He thought he would have to leave San Francisco's urban setting to find nature.

In 1990 Bittner did not feel as if he was achieving his goals, though he sometimes bicycled 180 miles a day. To relax, he watched the butterflies and birds in the garden, and one day he spotted four parrots among the birds that came by. By fall he had spotted a dozen parrots. When he moved higher up the hill to be resident house care-taker, he discovered that twenty-six parrots would arrive at the same time.

Neighborhood residents who often saw the tropical green birds with bright red heads wheeling together and screeching excitedly noted that the green-feathered parrot flock was increasing. But only Bittner took the time to research what species of colorful birds were showing up beside house finches, mourning doves, and scrub jays when he put wild birdseed out on his fire escape. The cherry-headed and blue-crowned conures, two parrot species originally from Ecuador and Peru, ate only sunflower seeds from his birdseed mixture. Bittner was fascinated with the interaction between the parrots as he obliged them with sunflower seeds: First three parrots and then gradually the whole flock arrived to eat.

He got to know the birds' individual personalities and gave them names like Connor (conure), Marlon (after Brando), and Ginsberg and Snyder after beat poets. Some even landed on his head or arms and allowed him to feed them. In his journal Bittner recorded each parrot's behavior, preferences, and actions when it arrived for three to four daily sunflower-seed feedings. He would watch the flock fly in the morning and discover which bird was accepted or cast out by the group and identified couples that would eventually mate.

Bittner also discovered that the conures' favorite nesting tree was another import to California—the Canary Island date palm. Over the years as the flock grew, he watched the several-month-old conures fledge in early September and fly away from the nests when they were big enough to be spotted. Even with little money, he doctored those that became ill as best he could and suffered as favorite conures died or failed to return with the flock.

As he bicycled around town, Bittner found that his parrots flew between the Ferry Building and the Presidio, but left in July to breed a few miles further south in Cole Valley and Parnassus Heights, not far from the University of California, San Francisco campus. He even spotted one bird near Mission Dolores. Perhaps the conures had escaped from a pet store or from owners who had bought the wild birds and, Bittner suspected, turned them loose when the birds bit and screamed.

Bittner soon decided that cross-mating between cherry-headed and blue-crowned conures created a new hybrid species. He tried to find out where the birds originated, but no one seemed to know for sure. And no one seemed to be documenting his flock. Some of the birds had bands that revealed only where they had legally passed through U.S. Customs.

Residents and tourists who climbed up Telegraph Hill noticed Bittner with the wild birds perched on him, or hanging upside down on a tree branch, flying and making noise nearby. People would ask him questions about the parrots. Even Bittner's hero, the Beat Generation poet Gary Snyder, hiked up the hill to see and talk to him about the parrots.

Telegraph Hill's birdman observed predators including hawks that would snatch, kill, and eat occasional flock members. Feral cats were a problem as well as humans who would inquire about capturing one of the wild parrots, possibly to sell them. Bittner was upset that people would think about trapping a wild creature.

As Bittner's living arrangements on Telegraph Hill became more tenuous, an award-winning documentary filmmaker, Judy Irving, called Bittner about a movie project she had in mind. She had heard about Bittner and the parrots. With some persuasion Bittner consented to be filmed with the wild parrots, introducing them, and describing the history, habits, and personality of each one. His passion for the birds he described as luminous in color, with behavior that was funnier than the Three Stooges, became Bittner's book and Irving's documentary, both named *The Wild Parrots of Telegraph Hill*. The book's subtitle was aptly stated as "A Love Story . . . with Wings."

The documentary film was released in early 2005. Bittner had mostly stopped feeding the flock that had grown to 160 when he realized that he now knew only a few by name. Other flocks of wild parrots were being identified in Southern California and in other states. There was at least one other separate flock in San Francisco.

Bittner and Irving became permanent residents of Telegraph Hill. Bittner's writing career was finally launched with his popular book.

The wild parrots of Telegraph Hill still stop by for an occasional feeding, and Bittner indulges them no more than once per day when he's home. The squawking flock of exotic bright-eyed green birds with fire-engine red or bright blue heads flashing by is no longer a mystery but one of San Francisco's newest tourist attractions.

GENDER TOGETHER

~ 2004 ~

SAN FRANCISCO'S YOUNG MAYOR WHO HAD BEEN in office only thirty-four days, and two elderly lesbians who had been committed to each other for fifty-one years were making history together on February 12, 2004. In a private San Francisco City Hall ceremony, Del Martin and Phyllis Lyon were declared "spouses for life" by San Francisco City Assessor Mabel Teng. A few minutes later the newlyweds were in Mayor Gavin Newsom's office receiving kisses from the man who had made it possible.

"I'm proud of you guys," beamed Newsom. "I don't know why it took me thirty-four days." The Martin-Lyon wedding was the first of 3,955 ceremonies performed for same-gender couples. They were granted same-sex marriage licenses by San Francisco County Clerk Nancy Alfaro: The mayor had cited the California constitution's equal protection clause in directing Alfaro on February 10 to "determine what changes should be made to the forms and documents used to apply for and issue marriage licenses in order to provide marriage licenses on a non-discriminatory basis, without regard to gender or orientation."

The county clerk's office staff changed the marriage application language from "man" and "woman" to "spouse" and "spouse." Then the gay rights community decided it was time to recruit *the* couple to make history in the United States' first government-authorized same-gender marriage.

Del Martin was eighty-three and Phyllis Lyon was seventy-nine. They had met in Seattle in 1950 when working on the same magazine and moved to San Francisco in 1953. By 1955 Martin, Lyon, and six other lesbians were tired of having nowhere to meet except bars and equally tired of social disapproval. They founded the Daughters of Bilitis and went public with their lifestyle and activism. Through the years they had been involved in lesbian rights campaigns, feminist organizations, and women's health care services.

On February 11 Martin and Lyon received a phone call at home in San Francisco's Noe Valley. The National Center for Lesbian Rights director inquired, "This will hopefully be the last thing the movement will ever ask you to do, but do you want to get married?"

After the Martin-Lyon wedding and with the Valentine's Day weekend fast approaching, city hall staffers scrambled to arrange paperwork and deputized more personnel to conduct weddings. Many city employees worked for free, while the county clerk's office waived fees for marriage ceremonies.

San Francisco City Hall rotunda's elegant, curved white marble staircase became the venue for almost 4,000 weddings during the next twenty-nine days. Outside the Beaux-Arts–style building with its gold-covered dome, gay and lesbian couples lined up around the block for hours with their children, families, and friends to sign the license and marry. Some people left work spontaneously and drove from Nevada and Oregon to get married. Even celebrities like Rosie O'Donnell arrived to support same-sex marriage by wedding her long-term partner. Florists from around the world sent bundles of flowers addressed "to any newlywed couple."

Some days it rained, and still the couples waited even without umbrellas. On March 11, one month after it all began, the Supreme Court of California ordered the same-sex marriages to stop immediately. On August 12, amid many lawsuits and countersuits, the same court ruled that the mayor had exceeded his authority and ordered all 3,955 marriages voided.

By March 2005 a San Francisco County Superior Court judge ruled that withholding marriage licenses from gays and lesbians was unconstitutional. The appeals would go on to the California Supreme Court, even as the California Legislature and voters took up the issue.

The whole world had been watching as San Francisco's young mayor acted in true San Francisco style: Do what you have to. Test the possibilities. Go to the frontier.

One year after their marriage, Del Martin and Phyllis Lyon were in a crowd of 3,000 people standing shoulder-to-shoulder, facing the marble staircase expectantly in the San Francisco City Hall rotunda. Many of the same-gender couples that had been married were there, too. There were cheers and applause as Mayor Gavin Newsom opened his arms and smiled. "Happy anniversary," he began.

SAN FRANCISCO FACTS & TRIVIA

Population: 776,733 (2004)

Incorporated: April 15, 1850

Origin of City Name: St. Francis of Assisi

Average Temperature: Low 42–55 degrees F; High 56–74 degrees F. Locals report temperatures close to 65 degrees F year-round.

Average Yearly Rainfall: 22.28 inches (but snow is rare)

City Colors: Black and gold

City Tree: 100-foot-tall Monterey cypress in front of McLaren Lodge, Kennedy Drive, Golden Gate Park

City Flower: Dahlia

City Bird: California quail

City Musical Instrument: Piano accordion

San Francisco's landmass is 46.7 square miles.

San Francisco is California's only combined city and county.

San Francisco Bay's average temperature is a chilly 55 degrees F.

Lombard Street, with a mere 21.3 percent grade, was dubbed "the crookedest street in the world" in 1923, but it is hardly San Francisco's steepest. Filbert Street between Leavenworth and Hyde Streets and Twenty-Second Street between Church and Vicksburg Streets tie for most precipitous with a 31.5 percent grade.

The Bay to Breakers 12-kilometer (7.46 miles) footrace from The Embarcadero through Golden Gate Park to the Pacific Ocean has been run annually since 1912. Each May 70,000–80,000 runners and wannabe runners, many in wacky costumes or teamed as thirteen-person centipedes, dance to live music en route and dodge each other while following a phalanx of seeded competitive runners.

The Sisters of Perpetual Indulgence first vamped in the Castro District in 1979; several men dressed in nun's habits appeared around the neighborhood and at local events. Firmly tongue in cheek, the racily-named and dressed "nuns" are social, political, and health activists with communities now in Europe and Australia.

The biotechnology industry began at a bar named Churchill's when investor and venture capitalist Robert Swanson, and University of California, San Francisco, biochemist and biophysicist Herb Boyer met for beers in 1976 and founded Genentech, Inc. to commercialize the insertion of DNA fragments into *E. coli* bacteria to produce specialized proteins.

Chinatown's Chinese Telephone Exchange switchboard operators had to speak five Chinese dialects and English from 1894 to 1949. They worked without telephone numbers to avoid unlucky numbers, connecting 12,000 subscribers whose names, addresses, and workplaces they had memorized.

The top of San Francisco City Hall's dome above the rotunda is 306 feet high; it was deliberately built to be taller than the 287.5-foot-high United States Capitol.

Though it is now inseparable from the skyline, many San Franciscans hated the Transamerica Pyramid when the 853-foot-high office tower went up in 1972. The forty-eight-story skyscraper, topped with a 212-foot spire, was designed to let more light into Financial District streets below.

"Yankee Clipper," "Joltin' Joe" DiMaggio, the famous New York Yankees baseball slugger, returned home to San Francisco's City Hall to marry rising film star Marilyn Monroe on January 14, 1954.

Dashiell Hammett wrote *The Maltese Falcon* when he lived at 891 Post Street. His fictional detective, Sam Spade, sleuths from an office that would have been at 111 Sutter Street. Narrow Burritt Street nearby bears a plaque inscribed: ON APPROXIMATELY THIS SPOT, MILES ARCHER, PARTNER OF SAM SPADE, WAS DONE IN BY BRIGID O'SHAUGHNESSY. The novel was published on Valentine's Day, 1930.

Baker Isidore Boudin's original sourdough starter that he brought to San Francisco in 1849 still makes one of the city's sourest French breads for Boudin Bakery. The secret ingredient in the paste "mother" dough made from flour and water is a bacterium that reproduces forever as long as it is kept wet at the right temperature.

Since 1981, when Friends of the Urban Forest started helping neighborhood residents plant and care for trees in front of their homes, the nonprofit has donated more than 35,000 trees, from purple-leaf plums, ficus, and gingko to Japanese flowering cherry trees.

In 1989 barking sea lions suddenly started hauling out onto the newly built K boat dock at Pier 39. The bayside shopping, dining, and entertainment mall with a seaside theme first tried to dissuade them, then abandoned the dock to the 600 to 900 sea lions that remain one of San Francisco's most popular tourist attractions.

San Francisco's flag includes a rising phoenix and the city motto: *Oro en Paz, Fierro en Guerra* (Gold in Peace, Iron in War).

Grant Avenue, Chinatown's main street, was known as Dupont Street, or Dupont Gai by Chinese until it was renamed for President Ulysses S. Grant in 1906. Dupont had been an officer on the USS *Portsmouth,* whose captain, John B. Montgomery, had raised the American flag at the customs house at San Francisco's main plaza in 1846. That plaza quickly became Portsmouth Square.

There is a Pet Cemetery at the San Francisco Presidio, with wooden grave markers and loving dedications to dogs, cats, and other companion creatures who have passed on.

Since 1854, when it was the West Coast's first Roman Catholic Cathedral, Old St. Mary's red brick clock tower, in Chinatown, has always warned in large letters: SON OBSERVE THE TIME AND FLY FROM EVIL!

For more than fifty years, San Francisco's population has remained close to 750,000, while the population of the nine counties in the San Francisco Bay Area region has boomed to six million inhabitants.

The mountains of the Sierra Nevada within Yosemite National Park provide 85 percent of San Francisco's water from the Hetch Hetchy Reservoir. Naturalist John Muir lobbied hard but failed to preserve the Yosemite Valley's sister valley, Hetch Hetchy, which was inundated with the waters of the Tuolumne River in 1934. The water is tunneled and piped 160 miles west for 2.4 million residents of the San Francisco Bay Area.

Built in 1870, the Old Mint at Fifth and Mission Streets was San Francisco's Granite Lady. One-third of U.S. gold was kept here in the 1930s.

The 75,398-acre Golden Gate National Recreation Area (GGNRA), also called the Golden Gate National Parks, is one of the world's largest urban national parks. San Francisco's Ocean Beach, Presidio, and Alcatraz are included as are Muir Woods National Monument's coastal redwoods and the Marin Headlands bluffs. Nineteen eco-systems protect endangered species like the northern spotted owl and California red-legged frog.

Masses of dahlias, San Francisco's city flower, bloom profusely in Golden Gate Park from July through September at the Conservatory of Flowers' Dahlia Dell.

Tony Bennett made the words "little cable cars climb halfway to the stars," from *I Left My Heart in San Francisco,* one of San Francisco's best-known refrains. Written by Douglass Cross and George Cory, it became one of two official city songs in 1969. The uplifting title song, *San Francisco,* from the 1936 film that starred Clark Gable and the songstress Jeanette MacDonald, became the second official city song in 1984.

BIBLIOGRAPHY

Cattle Drive—1776

Anza timelines, campsites, and daily logs Web site: anza.uoregon.edu/

Center for Advanced Technology in Education, University of Oregon. 1998–2003.

Garate, Don. Discoverers Web Web site: www.win.tue.nl/cs/fm /engels/discovery/anza.html

Langelier, John Phillip, and Daniel Bernard Rosen. *Historic Resource Study, el Presidio de San Francisco: A History Under Pain and Mexico, 1776–1846.* Denver Service Center: United States Department of the Interior, National Park Service, August 1992.

National Park Service, Presidio of San Francisco Web site: www.nps.gov/prsf/

Marsh to Mission—1777

Bean, Walton, and James J. Rawls. *California: An Interpretive History.* New York: McGraw-Hill Book Company, 1983.

Boulé, Mary Null. *California Native American Tribes: Ohlone Tribe.* Vashon, Wash.: Merryant Pubishers, Inc., 1992.

Emanuels, George. *California Indians: An Illustrated Guide.* Lemoore, Calif.: Kings River Press, 1994.

The Tragic Romance of Concha and Nikolai—1806

National Park Service, Presidio of San Francisco Web site: www.nps .gov/prsf/history/bios/concep.htm

Russian Web site on Commander Rezanov: rezanov.krasu.ru/eng/ commander

Wisconsin Historical Society Web site, *The Rezanov Voyage to Nueva California 1806:* www.americanjourneys.org/aj-128/index.asp#

Eureka! Golden Boomtown—1849

Altman, Linda Jacobs. *The California Gold Rush in American History.* New Jersey: Enslow Publishers, Inc., 1997.

Blumberg, Rhoda. *The Great American Gold Rush.* New York: Bradbury Press, 1989.

Ketchum, Liza. *The Gold Rush.* (Based on the Public Television series *The West.*) Boston: Little, Brown and Company, 1996.

Van Steenwyk, Elizabeth. *The California Gold Rush: West with the 49ers.* New York: Franklin Watts, 1991.

Blue Jeans—1853

Evans, Harold. *They Made America.* New York: Little, Brown and Company, 2004.

Fardon, G. R. *San Francisco in the 1850s: 33 Photographic Views by G.R. Fardon.* New York: Dover Publications, Inc., 1977.

Levi Strauss & Co. Web site: www.levistrauss.com

Justice at Fort Gunnybags—1856

Civil War Home Web site: civilwarhome.com/sherbio.htm

Eames, David B. *San Francisco Street Secrets.* Baldwin Park, Calif.: Gem Guides Book Co., 1995.

McGloin, John B., S. J. *San Francisco: The Story of a City.* San Rafael, Calif.: Presidio Press, 1978.

National Park Service, Vicksburg National Military Park Web site: www.nps.gov/vick/visctr/sitebltn/farragut.htm

Virtual Museum of the City of San Francisco Web site:
www.sfmuseum.net/hist1/vigil56.html
www.sfmuseum.net/hist6/corahang.html
www.sfmuseum.net/hist6/hang.html
www.sfmuseum.net/hist6/Sherman2.html
www.sfmuseum.net/hist10/shopkins.html

Fire Lady—1858

Firefighter's Real Stories Web site: www.firefightersrealstories.com/volunteer.html

San Francisco Fire Museum Web site: www.sffiremuseum.org

Soulé, Frank, Gihon, John H, M.D., and James Nisbet. *The Annals of San Francisco.* San Francisco, 1855. Republished in 1999 by Berkeley Hills Books.

Virtual Museum of the City of San Francisco Web site:
www.sfmuseum.net/hist1/h-coit.html
www.sfmuseum.net/hist1/h-coit2.html
www.sfmuseum.net/hist/helmet.html

Hallidie's Hill Climber—1873

Bacon, Daniel. "Riding and Remembering the Cable Cars of San Francisco with Daniel Bacon." *Hemispheres,* March 1996.

Bunnell, J. S. "Towed by Rail." *St. Nicholas Magazine,* November 1878.

Hallidie, A. S. "The Wire Rope Railways of San Francisco, California." *Scientific American Supplement,* September 17, 1881.

Joe Thompson's Cable Car Guy Web site: www.cable-car-guy.com

Svanevik, Michael, and Shirley Burgett. "How Hallidie's Invention Reshaped the Map of the City." *San Francisco Examiner,* October 14, 2001.

Nabobs of Nob Hill and the Spite Fence—1877

Lockwood, Charles. *Suddenly San Francisco: The Early Years of an Instant City.* San Francisco: The San Francisco Examiner Division of The Hearst Corporation, 1978.

PBS/WGBH American Experience Web site, *Transcontinental Railroad:* www.pbs.org/wgbh/amex/tcrr/peopleevents/

Richards, Rand. *Historic San Francisco: A Concise History and Guide.* San Francisco: Heritage House Publishers, 1991.

Virtual Museum of the City of San Francisco Web site: www.sf museum.net/hist1/rail.html

Le Roi Est Mort—1880

Chandler, Robert J. Letter to the editor: "A Bay Bridge by Another Name." *San Francisco Chronicle,* September 27, 2004.

Emperor Norton Bridge name Web site: www.emperornorton bridge.org/

Frank, Phil. *Farley* comic strip: Emperor Norton and the Bay Bridge. *San Francisco Chronicle,* September 2004–March 2005.

"Imperial Ashes: Decease of Norton I, Emperor of the United States." *San Francisco Chronicle,* January 8, 1880.

"Le Roi Est Mort." *San Francisco Chronicle,* January 9, 1880.

"Le Roi Est Mort: Imperial Norton is Dead and Turned to Clay." *San Francisco Chronicle,* January 11, 1880.

Virtual Museum of the City of San Francisco Web site: www.sfmuseum.net/hist1/norton.html

Cliffs, Baths, and Heights—1881

Jackson, Donald Dale. "Sutro's Stately Pleasure Dome." *San Francisco Chronicle, This World,* April 25, 1993.

National Park Service, Golden Gate National Recreation Area Web site: www.nps.gov/goga/clho/

Okamoto, Ariel Rubissow. *A Day at the Seaside: San Francisco's Sutro Heights, Cliff House, and Sutro Baths.* San Francisco: Golden Gate National Parks Association, 1998.

Virtual Museum of the City of San Francisco Web site: www.sf museum.net/sutro/bio.html

Rescue in Chinatown—1895

Asbury, Herbert. *The Barbary Coast: An Informal History of the San Francisco Underworld.* New York: A.A. Knopf, 1933.

Donaldina Cameron House Web site: www.cameronhouse.org/ history/

Evans, Albert S. *A la California: Sketch of Life in the Golden State.* San Francisco: A.L. Bancroft & Co., 1873.

Virtual Museum of the City of San Francisco Web site:
www.sfmuseum.net/1906/ew15.html
www.sfmuseum.net/hist9/cook.html

Shaking Inferno—1906

Barker, Macolm E., ed. *Three Fearful Days: San Francisco Memoirs of the 1906 Earthquake & Fire.* San Francisco: Londonborn Publications, 1998.

London, Jack. "Story of an Eyewitness." *Collier's Weekly,* May 5, 1906.

Morris, Charles, LL.D., ed. *The San Francisco Calamity by Earthquake and Fire.* Philadelphia: J.C. Winston Co., approx. 1906.

Virtual Museum of the City of San Francisco Web site:
www.sfmuseum.net/hist5/jlondon.html
www.sfmuseum.net/1906/06.html

Ellis Island of the West—1910

Angel Island Association Web site: www.angelisland.org

Angel Island State Park Immigration Station Historical Guide brochure. Tiburon, California, Angel Island Association.

McManis, Sam. "Guardian of Angel Island Memories." *San Francisco Chronicle,* January 26, 2001.

PBS/WGBH Web site, *Bubonic Plague Hits San Francisco:* www.pbs.org/wgbh/aso/databank/entries/dm00bu.html

Christmas Eve Diva—1910

Ashley, Tim. "Friends of the Girth." *The Guardian,* March 9, 2004.

Kates, Brian. "No sideways." *New York Daily News,* May 16, 2004.

KQED, Inc. Web site: www.kqed.org/w/sinfiregold/luisa.html

Virtual Museum of the City of San Francisco Web site:
    www.sfmuseum.net/bio/lotta.html
    www.sfmuseum.net/bio/luisa.html

Panama Connection—1915

Blaisdell, Marilyn. *San Francisciana Photographs of Three World Fairs.*
    San Francisco: Marilyn Blaisdell, 1994.

McGloin, John B., S. J. *San Francisco: The Story of a City.* San Rafael,
    Calif.: Presidio Press, 1978.

San Francisco Memories Web site: www.sanfranciscomemories
    .com/ppie/

Virtual Museum of the City of San Francisco Web site:
    www.sfmuseum.net/hist9/overfair.html
    www.sfmuseum.net/hist9/ppietxt1.html
    www.sfmuseum.net/hist10/scint.html

Death of a President—1923

Court TV's Crime Laboratory Web site: www.crimelibrary.com/
    terrorists_spies/assassins/warren_harding/

Evans, Harold. *The American Century.* New York: Alfred A. Knopf,
    1998.

Nolte, Carl. "California Century, Part 2: The Big Boom." *San Francisco Chronicle,* April 25, 1999.

Parrish, Michael E. *Anxious Decades: America in Prosperity and Depression, 1920–1941.* New York: W.W. Norton & Company, 1992.

Perrett, Geoffrey. *America in the Twenties.* New York: Simon and Schuster, 1982.

Bloody Thursday—1934

International Longshoremen's and Warehousemen's Union Web site: www.ilwu19.com/history/biography.htm

McGloin, John B., S. J. *San Francisco: The Story of a City.* San Rafael, Calif.: Presidio Press, 1978.

Radio Documentary: *"From Wharf Rats to Lords of the Docks: The Life and Times of Harry Bridges."* Producer: Ruskin, Ian for PRI (Public Radio International), 2001. Audio on KCRW Web site: www.kcrw.com/specials/harrybridges.html

Virtual Museum of the City of San Francisco Web site:
www.sfmuseum.net/hist/thursday.html
www.sfmuseum.net/hist/thursday2.html
www.sfmuseum.net/hist1/bund2.html
www.sfmuseum.net/hist1/rossi.html
www.sfmuseum.net/hist1/34strike.html
www.sfmuseum.net/hist4/maritime [maritime 1–23].html
www.sfmuseum.net/sfpd/sfpd5.html

China Clipper—1935

Evans, Harold. *They Made America.* New York: Little, Brown and Company, 2004.

Jablonski, Edward. *Man with Wings.* Garden City, N.Y.: Doubleday & Company, Inc., 1980.

Virtual Museum of the City of San Francisco Web site: www.sf museum.org/hist8/clipper.html

Bridging the Gate—1937

Horton, Tom. *Superspan: The Golden Gate Bridge.* San Francisco: Chronicle Books, 1983.

MacNamara, Mark, and David Weir. "Golden Gate Lies." *7X7SF,* Spring, 2002.

PBS/WGBH American Experience Web site, *Golden Gate Bridge:* www.pbs.org/wgbh/amex/goldengate/peopleevents/

van der Zee, John, and Russ Cone. "The Case of the Missing Engineer." *San Francisco Examiner Image,* May 22, 1992.

Internment Displacement—1942

Bean, Walton, and James J. Rawls. *California: An Interpretive History.* New York: McGraw-Hill Book Company, 1983.

California Digital Library, Online Archive of California Web site: www.oac.cdlib.org

Nichi Bei Bussan history Web site: www.nbstore.com/history.htm

Virtual Museum of the City of San Francisco Web site: www.sf museum.net/war/evactxt.html

The Beatniks "Howl"—1955

Ginsberg, Allen. *Howl and Other Poems.* San Francisco: City Lights Books, 1956.

Raskin, Jonah. *American Scream: Allen Ginsberg's Howl and the Making of the Beat Generation.* Berkeley and Los Angeles: University of California Press, 2004.

Waldman, Anne, ed. *The Beat Book.* Boston: Shambala Publications, Inc., 1996.

Un-American Hosing—1960

Evans, Harold. *The American Century.* New York: Alfred A. Knopf, 1998.

LaSalle, Mick. "He Was Blacklisted in a National Witch Hunt. Yet Writer Dalton Trumbo Never Lost His Integrity." *The San Francisco Chronicle,* March 3, 2005.

Rosenfeld, Seth. "The FBI's Secret UC Files" and "Trouble on Campus." *The San Francisco Chronicle,* June 9, 2002.

SLATE archives Web site: www.slatearchives.org

H'Ashbury Lov'In—1967

Cooke, Ariel Zeitlin. "Volunteer Doctor." *Diversion* magazine, April 2000.

Dr. Dave Smith Web site: www.drdave.org/Articles/April2000-Diversion.htm

Hinkle, Warren. "A Social History of the Hippies." *Ramparts* magazine, March 1967.

Radio Netherland Wereldomroep Web site: www2.rnw.nl/rnw/en/features/cultureandhistory/031221be-in.html

Virtual Museum of the City of San Francisco Web site:
www.sfmuseum.net/hist1/habib.html
www.sfmuseum.net/hist1/rock.html

La Raza Rising—1968

Galería de la Raza Web site: www.galeriadelaraza.org

Rena Bransten Gallery Web site: Rupert García: www.renabranstengallery.com/garcia.html

San Francisco State University Web site:
www.library.sfsu.edu/strike/chronology.html
www.sfsu.edu/~cecipp/cesar_chavez/chronolgy.htm
www.sfsu.edu/~100years/history/memories/memories.htm

Smithsonian Institution, Archives of American Art Web site:
www.aaa.si.edu/collections/oralhistories/transcripts/garcia96.htm

Invasion of Alcatraz—1969

California State University Long Beach, American Indian Occupation of Alcatraz Web site: www.csulb.edu/~gcampus/libarts/am-indian/alcatraz/

McMaster, Gerald, and Clifford E. Trafzer, ed. *Native Universe: Voices of Indian America.* Washington, D.C.: National Geographic Society and Smithsonian Institution, National Museum of the American Indian, 2004.

National Park Service Alcatraz Web site: www.nps.gov/alcatraz

Winton, Ben. "Alcatraz: Taking Back the Rock." *Native Peoples Magazine,* Fall 1999. Online at www.nativepeoples.com/article /articles/55/1/199-Fall.

Sunset Bank Robber—1974

CNN Web site: www.cnn.com/CNN/Programs/people/shows/hearst /profile.html

Court TV's Crime Laboratory Web site: www.crimelibrary.com/ terrorists_spies/terrorists/hearst

Hearst, Patricia Campbell. *Patty Hearst: Her Own Story* (originally published as *Every Secret Thing*). New York: Avon Books, 1988.

"Patricia Hearst Discusses Her Presidential Pardon." CNN. January 31, 2001.

San Francisco Independent "Heart of the City" columnist Hank Donat's Web site: www.mistersf.com/notorious/notpatty.htm

Murder at City Hall—1978

Herscher, Elaine. "The Moscone-Milk Killings, 20 Years Later." *San Francisco Chronicle,* November 27, 1998.

Mungo, Ray. *San Francisco Confidential.* New York: Birch Lane Press, 1995.

Shilts, Randy. *The Mayor of Castro Street.* New York: St. Martin's Press, Inc., 1982.

Uncle Donald's Castro Street Web site: thecastro.net/milk/white night.html

Parrots on Telegraph Hill—1990

Bittner, Mark. *The Wild Parrots of Telegraph Hill.* New York: Harmony Books, 2004.

Irving, Judy, film producer, director. "The Wild Parrots of Telegraph Hill," 2005.

Mark Bittner's The Wild Parrots of Telegraph Hill Web site: www.pelicanmedia.org/wildparrots.html

Thornton, Carla. "Friend of the flock: Mark Bittner and the parrots of Telegraph Hill." Parrot Chronicles: The online magazine for parrot lovers, March-April 2003. www.parrotchronicles.com/marchapril2003/parrotpeople.htm

Gender Together—2004

Hampton, Adriel. "Most Gay Couples Decline City Refund." *San Francisco Examiner,* December 21, 2004.

Hull, Anne. "Just Married, After 51 Years Together, Activist Gay Couple Accepts Leading Role." *Washington Post,* February 29, 2004.

Marech, Rona. "Joy, Gratitude Mark Anniversary of San Francisco's Gay Marriages."April 23, 2005. *San Francisco Chronicle,* February 13, 2005.

———. "Inside View of City Hall's Same-sex Marriage Drama." *San Francisco Chronicle,* April 23, 2005.

INDEX

ABOUT THE AUTHOR

San Francisco-based Maxine Cass has history and medieval studies degrees from the University of California, Santa Barbara. After Peace Corps Volunteer service in Senegal, she began a journey of self-discovery while photographing, researching, and writing books and articles on San Francisco, the Western United States, Canada, Florida, and Mexico.